CSR

Activities and Community Development in India

Prashant Kumar Pandey
Sukanta Kumar Baral

Qurate
quratebooks.com

CSR

Activities and Community Development in India

Prashant Kumar Pandey
M.Com, Ph.D.
Research Scholar, Department of Commerce, Faculty of Commerce & Management, Indira Gandhi National Tribal University, Amarkantak, Madhya Pradesh, India

Sukanta Kumar Baral
M.Com, LL. B, MBA, Ph.D.
Professor, Department of Commerce, Faculty of Commerce & Management, Indira Gandhi National Tribal University, Amarkantak, Madhya Pradesh, India
https://orcid.org/0000-0003-2061-714X

Published by Qurate Books Pvt. Ltd.

Published in 2023

ISBN: 978-81-19263-63-9

Qurate Books Pvt. Ltd.
Goa 403523, India
www.quratebooks.com
Tel: 1800-210-6527, Email: info@quratebooks.com
Printed at Manipal Technologies Limited, Manipal

Preface

A prosperous nation required prosperity in society and community, a community where development norms were met, such as a good health care system, youth development, sufficient sanitation facilities, a developed education system, and a healthy environment, among other things.

In the Indian context, community development was a serious issue with numerous contributing factors, such as a large population, widespread illiteracy, extreme poverty, the nation's long history of servitude (more than 800 years), a lack of natural resources, etc. Since independence, both the central and state governments have implemented numerous policies in accordance with the needs of the state for the development of society and community. However, due to political pressure, the financial crisis, the high population, community pressure, natural calamities, etc., the community development target was still not met.

For the development of nation and society as well business organizations also contribute in the form Corporate Social Responsibility (CSR) Traces of concept of CSR was old as old concept of business and industry, evidence of that was found in ancient literature but identity was different like Daan, Dasant, Jakat, Trusteeship etc. Modern CSR was created in the west as a result of the industrial revolution, and it quickly spread to India as a result of colonial rule and market globalisation. Prior to 2013, CSR was not required, but India changed the course of CSR history by enacting Section 135 of the Companies Act 2013 and making CSR mandatory there. Following India, several other nations followed suit, there were established rules and conditions for mandatory CSR activities in the Indian context. Today's CSR idea is well known as an organization's responsibility to society, where organisations are accountable for the effects of their actions on the environment and society. Organisations are also responsible to their stakeholders, including the environment, society, and the human resources within the organisation. CSR is vitally important to the government's goal of sustainable development.

CSR is an organization's commitment to behave and function responsibly while keeping its stakeholders' interests in mind. CSR is simply not an altruistic activity in today's globalised world. Its company strategy encourages both commercial and social engagement. Many smart firms develop a proper CSR strategy and see it as a critical activity in addition to marketing, production, and investment. Numerous global studies have found that organisations with effective CSR strategies have better levels of consumer loyalty, improved financial performance, increased market share, and goodwill.

In this approach, community development is necessary for the general growth of the country. Governments take many steps in this direction, but they fall short of the desired results. Therefore, through CSR, business organisations also contribute to the advancement of the country and society. Activities related to corporate social responsibility are crucial for the advancement of society and the community, as well as being highly advantageous for the organisations. Additionally, the current study aims to look into the various facets of corporate social responsibility and its significance. This book investigates a number of related facts and concerns in regard to CSR initiatives and their community impact in Indian states, particularly Madhya Pradesh and Chhattisgarh.

Authors

Acknowledgements

One of the most difficult issues for humanity this century is how to achieve sustainable, just, and balanced development. Current and future generations' demands cannot be satisfied unless natural systems and international norms preserving key social and environmental values are respected. In this setting, it is becoming increasingly clear that the role of CSR is important to contribute to the resolution of shared community problems. Strategically, businesses can only thrive when the communities and ecosystems in which they operate are in good health, education and other related issues.

The completion of this thesis benefits from the active guidance and imaginative direction of Prof. S. K. Baral, the Ph.D. Supervisor, who is an easygoing and open-minded teacher; without his inspiration and guidance, it would not be able to finish the thesis on time and give the scholar a Ph.D. degree. Apart from all of him, Prof. S.S. Bhadouria, HoD, Commerce and DRC Chairman, Prof. A. P. Singh, Dean FoC&M, Prof. Ajay Wagh, Prof. Ashish Mathur, Dr. Satish Modi, Dr. M Sanjoy Singh, Dr. H.S. Vinchu, Dr. V.K. Dixit and all other esteemed teachers of the FoC&M who have provided their valuable advice and suggestions throughout the research journey. It goes without saying that we are grateful to all co-research scholars for their continuous encouragements. Nevertheless, the administration of Indira Gandhi National Tribal University (A Central University), Amarkantak, Madhya Pradesh, has extended its support to accomplish the scholar's ambition, for which we thank everyone directly and indirectly concerned.

Further, those who provided thorough and critical input on the thesis were encouraged to clarify concepts, research specific aspects of insight work, and explain the reasoning behind certain proposals. We would also want to thank the numerous people who have assisted us in understanding and applying the art and science of CSR, as well as its societal ramifications and community effect in Indian states, particularly Madhya Pradesh and Chhattisgarh.

Authors

Contents

List of Tables

List of Acronyms and Abbreviations

CSR	Corporate Social Responsibility
CD	Community Development
GDP	Gross Domestic Profit
SDG	Sustainable Development Goal
YD	Youth Development
WBCSD	World Bank Committee for Sustainable Demand
LPG	Liberalization Privatization Globalization
HBR	Harvard Business Review
CED	Committee for Economic Development
FDI	Foreign Direct Investment
ILO	International Labor Organization
ISO	International Standard Organization
HR	Human Resources
SHG	Self Help Group
N.G.O.	Non-Government Organization
R.O.I.	Return on Investment
G.C.G.	Good Corporate Governance
α	Cronbach's Alpha
CFP	Corporate Financial Performance
CSP	Corporate Social Performance

CHAPTER- 1

Introduction

"The Business of business should not be about money. It should be about responsibility. It should be about public good, not private greed".

- *Anita Roddick*

Corporate Social Responsibility (CSR) is the responsibility of the Organization toward Society, and employees contribute to their quality of life. Corporate social responsibility is also called corporate awareness, corporate citizenship, or responsible business; it is a company or organization's corporate self-regulation policy.

According to World Bank Committee for Sustainable Development (WBCSD, 1998), "*The continuing commitment by a business organization to behave ethically and contribute to economic development while improving the quality of life of work force and their families as well as local community and society at large.*"

1.1 BACKGROUND OF CSR

After the end of the Second World War, the Cold War, and the break-up of the Soviet Union. The world Has come into in new era where most Countries opened their economy and offered opportunities for Investment worldwide at that time. India Also adopted the policies of LPG (Liberalization, Privatization, and Globalization). This Globalization process provides opportunities for developing countries to participate in Cultural affairs and Socio-economic Affairs Globally. Complete access to the market, investment opportunities, and the promise of transfer of technology increase the productivity and living Standard among Developing Countries. With new opportunities of Globalization, Some Challenges are raised like Inequality within the nation abroad, Forest Degradation, and financial Volatility. Overcoming these problems has increased the Practice of Corporate Social Responsibility (CSR).

Corporate Social responsibility is the promise of a Business Organization to establish a balance between financial performance and quality of life of its workforce and their family, the Surrounding Environment, and the welfare of Society at large, to Gain legal Compliance, Values Globally and sometimes social efforts. Organizations include no activities and practices in his CSR policies like Donation, Charitable Activities, Welfare activities and many more to address issues of labour laws and human rights. CSR practice of every organization may be different; it depends upon many crucial factors like Company Size, Type of organization, Country laws, and many more.

Corporate Social Responsibility may be defined as a Business Strategy that meets the organization's expectations of legal compliance, ethical and public have. The recent two-decade mutual relationship among business entities, Society, and the state was changed (Edenkcamp, 2002). Corporate Social Responsibility has become prominent in the Indian Scenario in recent decades because business organizations realized that sustainable and trustworthy relations with the Community and Society significant play a vital role in the sustainability and growth of the business; this is also a key driver for motivating them for CSR (Ramya Satish, 2010). CSR has come out of the bracket of doing social good, and it has become a business necessity because organizations realize that what is important for Society, workers, and the Environment is also good te Social Responsibility. Carroll seeks the d Business organizations and states how to sibilities.

ial responsibility, different thing and act is f preference of framework is the "Action phase onding in social sphere" called by Carroll, Corporate Social Performance (CSP). Social and Corporate Auditing are other concepts 1870 between 1980. In the eighties, many efforts e this concept differently, like policies, principal, th E. Goodpaster of Harvard Business School ept called Corporate Conscience.

erick, explained in the mid of 1986, he challenged that time and argued that everyone was failing ess and societal expectations; he described the f CSR with two different aspects first one is cial Responsibility, and the second one is Corporate siveness (how to respond with issues). He motivates ness leaders to look deep into the normative function . He strongly believes in a merger of business ethic ate responsibilities, and this may call the third wave o ined as Corporate Social Rectitude. Recently Corporat lity Gained Some think tanks and Scholars now focu zations' accountability towards their stakeholders. No are continuously trying to define, redefine and clarif ept. In recent years, they tried to disparate principles an into a comprehensive Structural model.

ourney of Corporate Social Responsibility

iversal Journey of CSR: Environmental and Social concer iness have a long history that is old as business and trad been traced those 5000 years back we have the commerci and operations to protect the forest. Around 1700BC, King opotamia Hammurabi introduced a law that if anyone died major inconvenience occurred in Society due to any Builde

for the organization (Indu Jain, 2010). Since the Nineties, CSR practices and policies have been drastically changed, and the working area was also expanded; the global standard for code of Conduct for CSR and their principal also helped increase the productivity and importance of CSR for Society and organizations.

Corporate Organizations have played a vital role in developing rural areas those out of government development practice and work for the Sustainability of an environment as well. In recent years due to increasing globalization and ecological issues, perception regarding the role of business organization has changed; now Corporate sector feel as an integral part of Society and accordingly act beyond their financial and legal boundaries, So they shift themselves from the mindset of pure profit to profit after social responsibility (KPMG and ASSOCHAM, 2008).

1.1.1 Origin and History of Corporate Social Responsibility

Although the concept of Corporate Social Responsibility has been well recognized in recent years, its Core idea can be recognized by its history. In the eighteenth Century, Business organizations realized the importance of an efficient workforce, and they lacked proper food, housing, and living standards, negatively impacting their workforce. Accessible medical facilities, Subsidized housing, and food seemed to a philanthropic activities of business organizations in those days (Brown 2005). In the 18th century, financial investment in CSR activities seemed optimistic. History of Corporate Social Responsibility highlights how academic scholars and business leaders Conceptualized and defined corporate Social Responsibility. Primary research of this envisioned project revealed the number of opinions and continuous efforts to articulate the responsibility of business, provide a philosophical foundation for those responsibilities, and develop how those responsibilities are effectively implemented. There were a few examples of development Journey.

Dempsey and David: before 1948, the term business responsibility was not used for the first time in1949; In an article published in Harvard Business Review (HBR), "The roots of Business Responsibilities" by Bernard Dempsey in this article this term is used and provides a philosophical foundation to this concept. After two months of this publication, one more author, Donald k. David published an article titled " Business responsibilities in an uncertain world." David called the business leaders to engage in public interest affairs from the immediate economic activity as they contribute to Society.

Dempsey provides the foundation of the concept, and his argument was based on these four concepts of Justice 1. Exchange Justice (The underlying trust exchange in the market). 2. Distributive Justice (the just relationship between organization and Government) 3. Genral Justice (Acceptance of legal framework beyond the ethical obligation) 4. Social and Contributed Justice (the obligation to contribute to the well-being of individuals and Society at large).

Dempsey and David explain why the corporate organization must contribute to public welfare 1. Because Businesses or human beings can sustain in a vacuum, all of them need a society that is well-functioning for their sustainability and progress. 2. And the second argument is that business organizations have many sustainable resources and capacity for the progress of the Society and well-being of an individual.

David outlines the Business organization's aims in this manner. 1. The company's operations must be efficient. 2. Organisations must be healthy in order for society to be healthy. 3. Act in this manner and contribute to society and other organisations. He also adds the idea that competition must be healthy and fair, and that the economic structure must work for justice and the well-being of society.

Morrell Heald, tried to write the history of Corporate Social Responsibility (CSR) between 1900 to 1960 titled that as "The Social Responsibility of Business- Company and Community 1900-1960" (Published in 1970). Heald focuses on the theory of Organizational responsibility but also argues that "Business should themselves

define his
that th
century
this trus
published
1906, Yale'
organization
so they align
in 1920 concep
Owen D. Young
Electric compan
between Organiza

Archie Carroll, t
definition of CSR bei
the views of eminen
between 1950-90 like C
and the committee of ec
Sethi, and many more. Au
Mr. Howard R Bowen c
Responsibility by Carroll. E
the concept of Business Sc
Social Responsibility as the '
those policies, actions, and deci
the objectives and values of our
Milton Friedman's concept of "I
means Businesses have only the
shareholder values and profitability.

Carroll also noted a definition o
Development (CED),1971; this co
Business function by public consent, an
the needs of society constructively to the

CED advocates for overlapping respo
financial issues to emerging non-financial o
where he also includes all these things lik
discretionary responsibilities. Carroll said th

is the heart of Corpor
attention of Scholars a
deal with social respon

Talking about soc
different. The phase
of management res
which also may cal
issue management
developed between
were made to defi
and ethics. Kenn
developed a conc

William Fred
the scholars of
between busin
terminology
Corporate So
Social Respo
eminent bus
and conflict
with corpor
CSR he de
accountab
on organi
scholars
the conc
activitie

1.1.2 J
Un
of bu
It ha
laws
Me
any

for the organization (Indu Jain, 2010). Since the Nineties, CSR practices and policies have been drastically changed, and the working area was also expanded; the global standard for code of Conduct for CSR and their principal also helped increase the productivity and importance of CSR for Society and organizations.

Corporate Organizations have played a vital role in developing rural areas those out of government development practice and work for the Sustainability of an environment as well. In recent years due to increasing globalization and ecological issues, perception regarding the role of business organization has changed; now Corporate sector feel as an integral part of Society and accordingly act beyond their financial and legal boundaries, So they shift themselves from the mindset of pure profit to profit after social responsibility (KPMG and ASSOCHAM, 2008).

1.1.1 Origin and History of Corporate Social Responsibility

Although the concept of Corporate Social Responsibility has been well recognized in recent years, its Core idea can be recognized by its history. In the eighteenth Century, Business organizations realized the importance of an efficient workforce, and they lacked proper food, housing, and living standards, negatively impacting their workforce. Accessible medical facilities, Subsidized housing, and food seemed to a philanthropic activities of business organizations in those days (Brown 2005). In the 18th century, financial investment in CSR activities seemed optimistic. History of Corporate Social Responsibility highlights how academic scholars and business leaders Conceptualized and defined corporate Social Responsibility. Primary research of this envisioned project revealed the number of opinions and continuous efforts to articulate the responsibility of business, provide a philosophical foundation for those responsibilities, and develop how those responsibilities are effectively implemented. There were a few examples of development Journey.

Dempsey and David: before 1948, the term business responsibility was not used for the first time in1949; In an article published in Harvard Business Review (HBR), "The roots of Business Responsibilities" by Bernard Dempsey in this article this term is used and provides a philosophical foundation to this concept. After two months of this publication, one more author, Donald k. David published an article titled " Business responsibilities in an uncertain world." David called the business leaders to engage in public interest affairs from the immediate economic activity as they contribute to Society.

Dempsey provides the foundation of the concept, and his argument was based on these four concepts of Justice 1. Exchange Justice (The underlying trust exchange in the market). 2. Distributive Justice (the just relationship between organization and Government) 3. Genral Justice (Acceptance of legal framework beyond the ethical obligation) 4. Social and Contributed Justice (the obligation to contribute to the well-being of individuals and Society at large).

Dempsey and David explain why the corporate organization must contribute to public welfare 1. Because Businesses or human beings can sustain in a vacuum, all of them need a society that is well-functioning for their sustainability and progress. 2. And the second argument is that business organizations have many sustainable resources and capacity for the progress of the Society and well-being of an individual.

David outlines the Business organization's aims in this manner 1. The company's operations must be efficient. 2. Organisations must be healthy in order for society to be healthy. 3. Act in this manner and contribute to society and other organisations. He also adds the idea that competition must be healthy and fair, and that the economic structure must work for justice and the well-being of society.

Morrell Heald, tried to write the history of Corporate Social Responsibility (CSR) between 1900 to 1960 titled that as "The Social Responsibility of Business- Company and Community 1900-1960" (Published in 1970). Heald focuses on the theory of Organizational responsibility but also argues that "Business should themselves define his responsibility and experience it." Heald experienced that the 'Trusteeship concept" began in the third decade of the century before Second World War. Andrew Carnegie introduced this trusteeship or stewardship concept in his article "Wealth," published in Journal called North American review in1889. In 1906, Yale's precedent Mr. Arthur Hadley addressed the Business organization and said that they are also a trustee of social interest, so they align a sense of responsibility with ethics accordingly. Then in 1920 concept of trusteeship was boldly introduced and applied by Owen D. Young, chairman, and Gerard Swope, president of General Electric company; Yong and Swope Constructed the relationship between Organization, workforce, Society, and State.

Archie Carroll, tried to provide an overview of the meaning and definition of CSR before the Second World War. He tried to examine the views of eminent professionals, scholars, and academicians between 1950-90 like Clarence Walton, Keith Davis, Howard Bowen and the committee of economic development, Dona woods, Parkash Sethi, and many more. Author of "Responsibilities of Businessman" Mr. Howard R Bowen declared as Father of Corporate Social Responsibility by Carroll. Because the first time his book dealt with the concept of Business Social Responsibility, Bowen explained Social Responsibility as the "Obligation of businessmen to pursue those policies, actions, and decisions which are desirable in terms of the objectives and values of our society." In his note, Carroll quoted Milton Friedman's concept of "Fundamentally Subversive," which means Businesses have only the responsibility of enhancing the shareholder values and profitability.

Carroll also noted a definition of the Committee of Economic Development (CED),1971; this committee defines CSR as " Business function by public consent, and its basic purpose is to serve the needs of society constructively to the satisfaction of the society."

CED advocates for overlapping responsibilities from hard core financial issues to emerging non-financial ones. Carroll defines CSR where he also includes all these things like; legal, economic, and discretionary responsibilities. Carroll said that Economic function is the heart of Corporate Social Responsibility. Carroll seeks the attention of Scholars and Business organizations and states how to deal with social responsibilities.

Talking about social responsibility, different thing and act is different. The phase of preference of framework is the "Action phase of management responding in social sphere" called by Carroll, which also may call Corporate Social Performance (CSP). Social issue management and Corporate Auditing are other concepts developed between1870 between 1980. In the eighties, many efforts were made to define this concept differently, like policies, principal and ethics. Kenneth E. Goodpaster of Harvard Business School developed a concept called Corporate Conscience.

William Frederick, explained in the mid of 1986, he challenged the scholars of that time and argued that everyone was failing between business and societal expectations; he described the terminology of CSR with two different aspects first one is Corporate Social Responsibility, and the second one is Corporate Social Responsiveness (how to respond with issues). He motivates eminent business leaders to look deep into the normative function and conflicts. He strongly believes in a merger of business ethics with corporate responsibilities, and this may call the third wave of CSR he defined as Corporate Social Rectitude. Recently Corporate accountability Gained Some think tanks and Scholars now focus on organizations' accountability towards their stakeholders. Now scholars are continuously trying to define, redefine and clarify the concept. In recent years, they tried to disparate principles and activities into a comprehensive Structural model.

1.1.2 Journey of Corporate Social Responsibility

Universal Journey of CSR: Environmental and Social concerns of business have a long history that is old as business and trade. It has been traced those 5000 years back we have the commercial laws and operations to protect the forest. Around 1700BC, King of Mesopotamia Hammurabi introduced a law that if anyone died or any major inconvenience occurred in Society due to any Builders, innkeepers, or former, they also go for death penalties. In1622, Dutch East India company's shareholders Distributed pamphlets and complained about the company's decisions and self-enrichment policies. With globalization and industrialization, this concept was also changed; corporate organizations of that era started philanthropic activities to overcome the impact of industrialization on Society and the Environment. Wallace B. Donham, Dean of Harvard Business School in 1929, delivered a speech and said that business history is a much older but present business model different from ancient, so the new business era has the responsibilities towards upcoming generations.

Almost eighty years ago, we experienced that is true; today, we face the same problem as education, food, and environmental problems Mr. Donham addressed.

In the words of Archie B. Carroll history of CSR is long back; it started in the 20th century; it is a continuous process that started from 1950 to now; we are working on that. Today the modern business world is more popular and appreciated, but there have been shreds of evidence that business was concerned about Society. The industrial revolution of the 1800s helped in emerging this concept before corporate business formation, known as Social Responsibility (SR).

Formalization of Corporate Social Responsibility is a product of the consistent effort of last century scholars, especially from the last 50 years; we have seen the evidence from all over the world but mainly in developed countries; most early writing evidence is found in the US (Covrou,1999).

In the last decade, the CSR concept was prevalent in European countries. Europe took it seriously and popularized it through formal writing, Seminar, Conferences, and other activities. Recently Asian Countries are also interested in CSR; many shreds of evidence have been found from different time periods in different countries, but if we focus on the concept's history, then we must consider the development pattern of the US and Europe.

Journey of CSR India: India was a vibrant country in ancient times, which means it has developed Society, commerce, and industry. India exporting all over the world, and evidence of the CSR concept was also found in different from of various time periods in ancient literature and religious Literature. Followers of Islam are doing charity or donation called "Zakat," which was used for the deprived section of Society; Hindus have followed the principle of "Dharmada," that also for the poor people of Society. Like this, Sikhs donate ten percent of their earnings called" Daashaant." All the Religious and Philosophical literature also proves the same concept. In the Fourth Century, a Hindu priest Kautilya wrote a book called 'Arthsastra' where he clearly explained the trade, commerce, agricultural Pattern, and other relevant things of that era. Jota Story or Mahabharat and other literature also explain the development of trade and industry.

In modern times, most business organizations believe that business is not only for money creation for their shareholder or owner, but they also have great responsibility towards Society. Pioneers of Indian Industry, many corporate houses like TATA, BIDLA, and BAJAJ also think like that. Founder of TATA, Mr. Jamshedji Nausrwan Ji Tata, expressed his views in 1903 "*We generate the wealth of for the nation, which comes from people must extent possible therefore get back to the people.*" Gandhi Ji also expressed his views on this topic, talking about moral responsibility and trusteeship of Society. He thinks that the capital holder is the trustee of Society; he may hold the resources and produce the product and services for the development of Society.

Mr. Jamanlal Bajaj, the founder of Bajaj Group, once said, "*Our wealth must be utilized for the development of society and nation, we should never fail to fail at least a portion of wealth to development of Social, economic, or educational development of the nation or for the province where we live.*"

1.1.3 Phase of CSR Development In India:

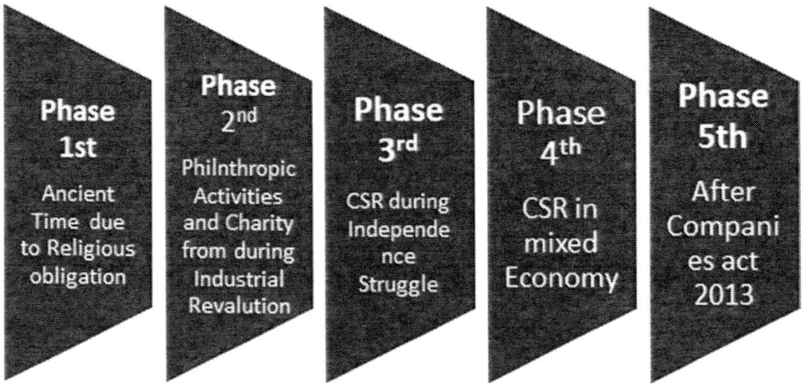

Figure 1. Different Phases of CSR Development in India
Source: Author's Compilation

CSR Development in Ancient Times

From ancient times India has had a vibrant culture, tradition, and philosophies; apart from this, India is very rich in wealth, trade, and industry. When we look at the history of Indian trade development, we find much evidence in our religious, philosophical, and ancient literature proving that CSR has existed in India for ancient but different reasons. At that time monarch was a businessman doing or supporting the welfare activities of Society because of religious obligation or fame. During that many works were done like the building of temples, digging of the pond, making well, construction of Salter house, Plantation of trees, Charitable and Donation activities was also performed during any kind of crisis and many more activities they performed which is purely for the service of Society and protection of Environment.

CSR during Industrial Revolution

The western industrial revolution reached India very soon because of colonial rule, which changed the scenario of the Indian CSR pattern. In Nineteenth-Century, few businesses like TATA, BIDLA, SINGHANIYA, BAJAJ, MODI, SHRIRAM, GODREJ, etc., few Strongly Support CSR as Philanthropic Activity (Mohan, 2011). Early pioneers of the Industrial economy was also the leaders of social welfare; it must be noted that CSR is not only motivated by the selflessly or religious reason but also due to cast base and political consideration for the development of Industry and Society. At that time, philanthropy and Charity mean they donate to supporting social welfare like schools, NGOs other religious Bodies without much effort and Engagement.

CSR During Independence Struggle

During Independence, Struggle CSR transformed into a new phase where Gandhi's concept of trusteeship was built up, and nation CSR activities followed accordingly. Companies were not working for social development as protest against colonial rule but were also involved in social and institutional development (Indian partnership forum, 2002). The business organization has the vision of modern and free India and works for that. At that time, the business organization was involved in constructing the school, college, and Research center and becoming their trustee (Mohan, 2011). Organizations merge their CSR program with Gandhi's vision of reform. Those programs are worked to abolish social abuses like un-touch ability, Rural Development, Women empowerment, etc.

CSR In Mixed Economy

After Independence and during the Cold war new era Indian Economy started. During that time, India opted for a mixed economy system where Capitalism and socialism existed together. After Independence, many legislative laws, environmental standards, labor laws, and License systems were imposed on Industries; these things also affected the CSR activities Pattern. During that time, the development of the private sector was reduced. On another side, new PSUs were established, and the public sector tried to equal the distribution of wealth. This is called the "Era of Command and Control"(Arora,2004). Imposing high taxes, quotas, and a license increased the malpractices among the organizations. The malpractice resulted in corporate governance, Community development, and environmental issues increasing and becoming political. There was an assumption that the public sector could tackle the issue of development, but the extent is limited to what was expected private sector grew and contributed to the Society and development of the nation. An initial step was taken by the politician, academician, and businessman at the national seminar on CSR in 1965 (Mohan, 2001).

After the eighties, Philanthropic activities were reduced, organizations were involved in mostly CSR activities, and a multi-stakeholder approach was introduced. In the Nineties, the Indian Government initiated new economic reforms, opened for all, partially abolished the license system, and became liberal in the sense of FDI. This step was to increase the CSR activities in the nation according to government expectations (Arora, 2004). Because of this, India became the leading actor in Globalization, and Transactional Corporations started global sourcing and became attractive production and manufacturing site. Western investors are more responsive to developing countries' environment and labor issues. Indian investors also started same way to comply with global standards.

CSR After Companies Act 2013

Corporate Social Responsibility (CSR) is Voluntary activity before the Companies act of 2013. However, after this act, it has become Compulsory in India Section 135 of the companies deals with it. India is the first country to make CSR legally compulsory, followed by the United Kingdom. CSR laws help transform excess capital from the have to charity. After this law, CSR investment increased by almost four-time. That also helps the organization take up the social, environmental, and economic activities to help the general populace.

Some pre-defined conditions obliged companies to contribute to CSR compulsory.

- The net worth of the company should be rupees 500 crores and more.
- Annual turnover must be more than 1000 crores or above.
- Net annual profit at least five cores.

If organizations meet the three conditions, CSR becomes compulsory for them. Furthermore, Company has to Construct a CSR committee.

** In the case of foreign companies above, Condition is applied with a slight change dealt with sec. 2(42)

1.2 STRUCTURE OF CSR COMMITTEE

- In the case of Public and listed companies, the CSR committee has at least three directors, one of which must be Independent.
- If the company is unlisted or private, there is no need for an independent director; two directors may be allowed.
- In the case of a foreign Company, two people were also allowed, but one of them must have an authorized residence in India sec.380(1)(d).

Companies Amendment act 2019: According to this act amendment, some points were included in the policy. Suppose the company fails to spend the CSR amount, then they have to transfer to another account with the nationalized bank within one month.

The company has only three years to spend unspent transferred money. If the company cannot spend that money, it must transfer the fund to Schedule VII of the act.

In case of violation, the active company may be fined a minimum of 50,000, which may extend up to 250,000. Furthermore, every defaulting officer of the company is liable for three years of Imprisonment and a 5 lakh fine, or it may be both.

1.3 MEANING AND DEFINITION OF CSR

Corporate Social Responsibility is a set of policies, actions, and programs integrated with business action, decision-making process, and supply chain, wherever the organization does business and includes responsibilities of past action and impact on future. In general terms, CSR means seeking to motivate companies to assume responsibility for problems and challenges addressed by the state.

The uniform definition of CSR is a matter of debate, but different scholars are trying to define it in their way.

Corporate Social Responsibility is not the only matter of public policy or legal compliance; organizations should also take Society's responsibility. In recent times, CSR has voluntarily integrated social and environmental concerns into their business practices and interaction with the stakeholders. Being a socially responsible Organization means doing more than legal compliance to improve Society.

"*CSR is the commitment of the business to contribute to sustainable economic development by working with employers, their families, the local community, and society at large to improve their quality of life, in ways that are both good for business and good for the development*" -World Business Council for Sustainable Development (WBCSD). Thus, the meaning of CSR has two-fold. On the one hand, it deals with the ethical behavior of the organization's stakeholders. In another hand deals sustainable development of Society.

Definition of Corporate Social Responsibility (CSR): Major factor of limited understanding of the CSR concept is its complexity and lack of consensual definition. CSR concept is widely discussed by many researchers, scholars, and academicians, but a universally accepted definition is yet to come. Different scholars, committees, and industrialists define corporate social responsibility differently. There are some definitions many researchers accept; academicians are as follows.

World Bank Committee for Sustainable Development (WBCSD,1998): "The Continue commitment by business to behave ethically and contribute to economic development while improving the quality of life of the workforce and their families as well as local Community and Society at large. "

International Labor Organization (ILO): Corporate Social Responsibility is a way in which enterprises give consideration to the impact of their operation on Society and affirm their principles and values both in their internal method and process and in their interaction with another actor. CSR is a voluntary enterprise-driven initiative and refers to the activities that are considered to exceed compliance with the law.

Carroll (2003): The social responsibility of business encompasses the economic, ethical, legal, and discretionary expectation that a society has an organization at a given time.

Mallenbaker (2004): CSR is about how companies manage their business process to produce an overall positive impact on society.

European Commission (2011): A concept whereby companies integrate social and environmental concern in their business operation and their interaction with their stakeholder voluntarily.

Bowen (1953): It refers to the obligation of the businessman to pursue policies, to make decisions or to follow lines of action which are desirable in terms of objective and values the society.

Committee for Economic Development (CED,1971): Business function by public consent and its essential purpose is to serve the needs of Society constructively to the satisfaction of the Society.

Eilbert and Parket (1973): Perhaps the best way to understand social responsibility is to think of it as 'good neighbourliness.' The concept involves two-phase. one is not doing anything which spoils neighbourliness. On the other hand, it may express a voluntary assumption to solve the neighbourliness problems.

Prakash Sethi (1975): Thus, Social Responsibility implies bringing corporate behavior up to a level where it is congruent with prevailing, social norms, values and expectation of performance.

Jones (1980): Corporate Social Responsibility is the notion the corporation has a responsibility to constituent groups in Society other than stakeholder and beyond that prescribed by law and union contract. Two facts of this definition are critical. First, the obligation must be adopted; behavior influenced by the coercive force of law and union contract is not voluntary. The second is broad, extending beyond the traditional duty of shareholder to other social groups such as customers, employees, suppliers and neighboring communities.

After analyzing the above definitions and many others, we can say that Corporate Social Responsibility (CSR) is a bunch of policies, programs, and actions resulting from overall organizational responsibility towards Society, stakeholders, and the Environment.

CSR is that responsibility that binds the organization to behave ethically, economically, and sustainably to fulfill the needs and expectations of Society, the State, and the Environment.

Corporate Social Responsibility is a duty or obligation towards its stakeholders like shareholders, Suppliers, workforce and their families, Society government, and the Environment also to work in a way that reduces the destructive impact of organizational activity and creates a sustainable environment for the upcoming generation and improve the quality life of present generation and Society at large.

1.4 MEASURING METHODS OF CSR

Measuring CSR activities is difficult because CSR policies and programs worldwide differ from country to country. So, there is no universal law or method to measure CSR, but many global organizations introduced some standards and principles to measure them. A brief introduction of some standards and principal are as follows:

ISO 26000: The ISO 26000 Standards set the standards and criteria for the concept of social responsibility published in 2010 by the International Organization for Standardization. These standards also provide guidance and proposals on implementing methodologies to start operating with socially responsible standards for different organizations (companies, NGOs, unions, etc.). Therefore, it is required to act ethically and transparently and contribute to Society's welfare by businesses with this credential.

Requirements for the ISO 26000

1. Scope
2. Terms and definitions
3. Understanding social responsibility
4. Principles of social responsibility
5. Recognizing social responsibility and engaging stakeholders
6. Guidance on social responsibility core subjects
7. Guidance on integrating social responsibility throughout an organization.

Fundamental Principals of ISO 26000

The Seven Key Principles, advocated as the roots of socially responsible behavior, are:

1. Accountability (ISO 8000)
2. Transparency
3. Ethical behaviour
4. Respect for stakeholder interests (stakeholders are individuals or groups who are affected by, or could impact, the organization's actions)
5. Respect for the rule of law
6. Respect for international norms of behaviour
7. Respect for human rights

The seven core issues to be addressed by all users of ISO 26000 are:

1. Organizational governance
2. Human rights
3. Work relations
4. Climate
5. Equal organizational practices

6. Consumer Issues
7. Community involvement and development

Global Reporting Initiatives

An agency or corporation publishes a sustainability report on its day-to-day work's cultural, environmental, and social impact. A sustainability report also presents the values and governance model of the organization, showing the connection between its strategy and its commitment to a sustainable global economy.

Sustainability reporting can help organizations assess, consider and communicate their economic, financial, social, and governance efficiency, and then set targets and manage change more effectively. A sustainability report is a central platform for communicating success and effects on sustainability–positive or negative.

Significant providers of sustainability reporting guidance include;

1. GRI (GRI's Sustainability Reporting Standards)
2. The Organization for Economic Co-operation and Development (OECD Guidelines for Multinational Enterprises)
3. The United Nations Global Compact (the Communication on Progress)
4. The International Organization for Standardization (ISO 26000, International Standard for social responsibility)

AA 1000: The AA 1000 Series came from the UK and was created by Accountability in 1999 to incorporate CSR aspects of management, auditing, and communication. An elaborate process that starts by recognizing stakeholder requirements and redefining values is the main feature of AA 1000.

Standard SGE 21: In 2000, for the first time, Forética, an international network of social responsibility developer organizations and professionals established in Spain, published the SGE 21 Company Standard. SGE 21 is the first social responsibility system in Europe to volunteer audit processes and obtain certification in Ethics and Social Responsibility for Management. The system includes quality and environmental models that enrich a multi-stakeholder vision.

The United Nations Global Compact Ten Principles, are explained below;

The United Nations Global Compact, initiated by UN Secretary-General, Kofi Annan, is another more comprehensive indicator of corporate contribution to social responsibility. Today, the Global Compact has been backed by 95 Indian businesses, marginally less than in Brazil but significantly more significant than in China on this point. The ten UN Global Compact principles, which are based on: the Universal Declaration for Human Rights, the International Labour Organization's Declaration on the Principles and Fundamental Rights at Work, the Rio Declaration on Environment and Development, and the United States, are widely accepted in all field of human rights, labor, and the Environment.

Human Rights

Principle 1: Businesses should support and respect the protection of internationally proclaimed human rights; and

Principle 2: Ensure they are not complicit in human rights abuses.

Labor

Principle 3: Businesses should uphold the freedom of association and effectively recognize the right to collective bargaining.

Principle 4: the elimination of all forms of forced and compulsory labor

Principle 5: the effective abolition of child labor; and

Principle 6: the elimination of discrimination in respect of employment and occupation.

Environment

Principle 7: Businesses should support a precautionary approach to environmental challenges.

Principle 8: undertake initiatives to promote greater environmental responsibility; and

Principle 9: encourage the development and diffusion of environmentally friendly technologies.

Anti-Corruption

Principle 10: Businesses should work against corruption in all forms, including extortion and bribery.

Other standards or principles

- The Global Compact of the United Nations
- The principles of "The Caux Round Table" (CRT)
- The Global Sullivan Principles
- SME Rating.

Corporate Social Responsibility guidelines of the Ministry of Corporate Affairs

Since this study seeks to understand the trends, issues, and strategies of CSR in India, the country's law or guidelines for implementing CSR become essential since most of the activities of the organizations are based on Govt Guidelines. Studies are also supported in the recommendations as a framework for analysis. Therefore, it is mandatory to refer to the Govt. Ministry of corporate affairs of India.

Fundamental Principle

Each company must formulate a CSR policy to guide its strategic planning and provide a roadmap for its CSR initiatives that are integral to overarching corporate policies and aligned with its corporate aims. The strategy should be formulated with the involvement of different executive-level members and should usually include the following core elements, approved by the Board and the CSR Strategy

Care for all Stakeholders: The businesses must respect, respond to and support all stakeholders, including shareholders, staff, clients, suppliers and, project stakeholders, Society as a whole. You will establish a mechanism to actively engage, track and minimize the inherent risks to all stakeholders.

Ethical functioning: Ethics, transparency, and accountability will help their governance structures. It would help if you did not indulge in coercive, unequal, unethical or anti-competitive business practices.

Respect for Workers' Rights and Welfare: Firms should provide a clean, stable, and fair work environment that values employee integrity. We must give all workers fair and non-discriminatory access to training and expertise to advance their careers. We should protect the freedom of association and adequate protection of the right to collective bargaining for jobs, have an adequate reparations system of complaints, not hire children and employees without prejudice for recruitment or employment, and ensure and retain equal opportunities without discrimination at all.

Respect for Human Rights: Companies should respect human rights for all and avoid complicity with human rights abuses by them or by the third party

Respect for Environment: Business action on pollution control and pollution reduction, waste collection, maintaining and minimizing, sustainable natural resource management, ensuring optimum resource management such as land and water usage, and proactively reacting to climate change issues by cleaner methods of production, encouraging effective use of resources and environmentally friendly technology.

Activities for Social and Inclusive Development: Companies should take on economic and social development activities in local communities and geographical areas, especially surrounding their operations, following their core competence and business interest. These may include education, building people's skills, health, social protection, etc., particularly in deprived sectors of Society.

Additional Instructions:

- CSR policy should provide an implementation plan that includes project tasks, establishing and monitoring observable physical goals, organizational structure, and responsibilities. Companies can partner with non-governmental organizations, local authorities, business organizations, and civil Society. We can influence the CSR supply chain and inspire people to volunteer social development efforts. They should develop a needs assessment and impact assessment program when conducting CSR operations in a specific field. Independent testing for selected pr may also be undertaken.
- In their CSR budgets, businesses can assign specific amounts. Tax profits may link this, expected CSR operations costs, or any other relevant parameter
- The company should engage in well-established and recognized programs and platforms that promote responsible business practices and CSR activities to share experiences and networks. That would help companies develop their CSR plans and effectively project a socially responsible picture.
- Through the website, annual reports, and other media, the organization will disseminate information on CSR strategies, programs, and development in a structured way to all stakeholders and the public at large.
- Project-based commitment in CSR should be complete and annual milestones should be reached at the beginning of each project.
- Specialized organizations and not staff, in general, shall carry out the project activities defined under CSR. Specialized

agencies may collaborate with other agencies separately or in tandem.

- Such specialized agencies would include formal or non-formal, local elected bodies such as panchayats, voluntary organizations (NGOs), schools, scholarships, trusts, missions, etc., self-help groups, states, semi-government and autonomous organizations, SCOPE, Mahila Mondays, Samiti and similar, Contracted public companies

1.5 BENEFITS OF CSR

In Early-Stage Corporate Social Responsibility is Religious or Philanthropic activity, and it is not compulsory. At that time, corporate organizations and people in business were only thinking about earning huge profits, increasing shareholder value, and maximizing the utilization of natural resources to earn profit.

However, with the time of modernization and globalization and due to industrial revaluation scenario will be changed. Due to globalization, many economies go through liberalization, and the industrial revolution increases the environmental issue. So, CSR activities play a crucial role in resolving all these environmental and societal problems.

Due to the importance of CSR, scholars, academicians, and other organizations started researching this to make it more valuable for Society. In that way, they introduced many models, theories, definitions, and policies. With time some Governments like India, the UK, etc., make it compulsory, and many more countries are thinking about that.

So here are some benefits of Corporate social responsibility discussed as follows:

Benefits for the organization: There are two types of benefits for the organization first are internal and external benefits.

Internal benefits: Organizations have some internal benefits those are as follows:

Employees Satisfaction: Yong employee of the organization expects more than the financial benefits. He wants some respect in Society and his workplace. He also wants to be a part of the decision-making process and other responsibilities apart from his regular job. A good CSR practice can help make employees happy and satisfied and attract new talents to be part of the organization.

Increase the Human resource productivity: There is a solid connection between CSR and employees' productivity because CSR fell them satisfied, and that increases productivity apart from satisfaction if an organization is seriously involved in CSR practices like environment protection, zero carbon emission, servicing to human resource and his family and Society as well. In this way, employees also adopt good habits that become healthy, motivated, and satisfied, so their efficiency and productivity will improve.

Reducing Expenses: If an organization follows the CSR norms, the organization also uses advanced technology to reduce pollution, also working with renewable energy or sustainable energy that also increases productivity and reduces the cost of production, and works for the wellness of Society, then the organization earns a reputation in Society and every employee to be part of that organization in that way recruitment cost also decreased.

Reducing Risk: Goodwill is the most valuable asset for the organization. The organization spent many years, much money, and effort to build a reputation in the market and Society. However, a small mistake can spoil all within a minute. If the company is serious regarding CSR activities, it also follows the rules and regulations of the state and does its business ethically; in this way, CSR has also reduced the risk to the organization.

External Benefits

Consumer Satisfaction: Responsible companies give their consumers greater priority with diminishing worldwide boundaries, customer knowledge of the conditions under which products and services are manufactured, and the effect on sustainability has become increasingly critical and demanding. CSR deals with the principles and duties that include people's behaviour. Most potential customers who carry out CSR initiatives expect similar services from their suppliers. The selection is sometimes dependent on the supplier's social reaction.

Improving access: Capital through high corporate management standards that educate investors regarding issues related to shareholder and stakeholder rights, accountability and disclosure, and proper governance systems. In her book The Sustainability Advantage, Bob Willard (2002): seven business cases benefiting from a triple fund are another significant example of CSR's business case.

Building Reputation: because of efficiency in CSR activities and improving environmental responsibility, and work for the deprived Society enhances the reputation in the Society and also recognition from the Government, Rating agencies, and other reputed other organizations.

Benefits for the Society: CSR focuses on the welfare of the Environment and Society at large. So, there are many benefits of Society as follows:

1) **Preservation of art and culture:** Many organizations have adopted policies to preserve the local heritage of the Society by supporting them. Provided job opportunities to local artists, and conducted training camps for their learning, helping promote that art by utilizing his machinery.

2) **Preservation of the Environment:** Environment protection is a burning issue in the modern era, so every organization and country focus on doing many things for the sustainability of the Environment. Now in CSR activities environment is a critical factor for that companies are doing many things they focus on the plantation, reducing deforesting, sustainable use of natural resources, water conservation, and renewable energy sources, etc., and make CSR strategies to attain this goal.

3) **Development of Infrastructure:** Business organizations also focus on developing infrastructure for the Society, like the building of the school, roads, plantations, healthcare centres, community centres, training centres, etc.; the organization provides the infrastructure to the Society.

4) **Creating employment opportunities:** The organization is performing many activities to create jobs through its CSR, such as providing training camps for the startup job seekers and transforming human resources from unskilled to skilled. Also,, financially support then new venture providing them seed capital and required training and support.

5) **Water Harvesting:** Water is being recovered, recycled, and reused efficiently to avoid water table loss in the industrial areas. Various rainwater harvesting units to utilize the rainwater, water treatment plants to treat the waste water, Water Supply in and around Plants on roads, toilets, horticulture activities, creating artificial lakes, etc., and drinking water supply to communities living in the neighboring areas through water tanks, pipelines, and tube wells.

6) **HR Development:** The safety of its employees and contractors has been the utmost priority for the Steel industry, as it is believed that by giving financial and economic support to one person, they are spreading happiness to one family. The safety, development & growth bring about a chain effect, which eventually connects to Society's development and holistic growth. Companies are rehabilitating villagers and providing them with the best resources as per the Government Policy.

7) **Sports & Culture:** Industries have been working at the grass-root level to bring out the best talent in all fields. Promoting young talent, giving them scholarships, awards, and training to develop their sporting skills have gone a long way to giving new champions to the nation. CSR teams

are constantly working to revitalize the local games and encourage more people to play.

8) **Promoting local Skills:** Much work is being done to revive and re-energize the handicraft units. Giving them market information, exploring new areas of technology, re-designing and rebranding the products to cater to the market demand, financial support, and training to harness their skills has given a lift to many dead handicraft units and families. We, the Steel industry, are committed to making dreams a reality, spreading smiles to millions, giving a helping hand, guiding and exploring the unseen within you, helping a girl fly high, ensuring a green tomorrow, to save a child within you, to be the light removing darkness and to spread happiness.

9) **Calamity Aid:** Industries have always been a trend setter in supporting people during natural calamities, and recently it has supported the construction of low-cost houses at Leh after a cloud burst. It provided galvanized sheets to Sikkim earthquake victims, contributed to Chief Minister's Relief Fund for aid to people affected by the Odisha floods, and provided flood relief packets during the floods in Uttar Pradesh.

10) **Vocational Training:** Villagers are provided vocational training in improved agriculture, mushroom cultivation, animal husbandry (goatery, poultry, fishery, piggery), achar/papad/agarbatti making, etc. Training is also provided for skill enhancement as welders, fitters, and electricians in sewing & embroidery, smokeless chulah making, etc. Vocational training centers like Bhilai Ispat Kaushal Kutir for rural and unemployed youth and Skill Development & Self Employment Training Institutes for the benefit of women and girls have also been set up.

11) **Youth Development:** Industries, as part of their corporate social responsibility, have taken up the initiative of rural training youth to either be absorbed by companies or start their work. Joining hands with Society for Rural

Industrialization (SRI), the government sector steel major has trained forty rural youths this season in carpentry, masonry, motorcycle, and pump set repair. Six of these have already been appointed by one of the leading motorbike brands for its workshop, whereas the remaining are striving to establish their enterprises.

1.6 COMMUNITY DEVELOPMENT

First and foremost, a community is generally defined as a group of individuals with a common goal who rely on each other to fulfill specific needs, live close to each other, and interact regularly. All group members have shared expectations, and the responsibility for these expectations is taken. The group takes the autonomy of other people in the Community equally and considerately. A sense of Community in one Community is defined as a sense of cooperation, commitment to the welfare of the group, willingness to communicate openly, and responsibility for oneself and others. The leader of the group is most important (Ismail,2009)

Compared to economic and Community development practice, the CD is a hybrid mechanism, plan, policy, and operation that can make a community sustainable. It may be perceived as a specific method of addressing, organizing, and constructing a social infrastructure in a given area. CD can be described as a process to challenge the extreme and unacceptable inequalities in conditions and infrastructures which influence the quality of life in the workplace. The process works better when the group has a sense of solidarity in all strata of society and citizenship (Community Glossary, 2009).

Community development is a proactive strategy or mechanism for resolving social change problems, allowing communities to discuss and work together on their shared values and problems (Lotz, 1977, p. 16). Hamilton (1992) identified community development in the order of priority decided by its increasing levels of competence as a planned and coordinated initiative that enables individuals to develop the attitudes, skills, and concepts necessary to engage directly in the practical solutions of the broadest range of issues of community improvement possible. Some characteristics of the community development process are the participation of community members in problem-solving and decision-making, a learning process aimed at changing behavior and requiring learning, and participants who improve their competence and ability to handle their affairs (Draper,1971). In terms of capacity-building, group growth and mobilization, and achievement of social, economic, cultural, and environmental goals, the performance of the community-based development process can be measured (Lovett, 1997).

Community development is a mechanism in which community members cooperate to solve everyday problems. Also, from this form of collective action taken at the grassroots level, community well-being (economic, social, climate, and cultural) emerges. The Community's growth ranges from a small group of small initiatives to large community initiatives.

Successful community growth should be a long-term, comprehensive and well-planned holistic, inclusive, and equitable initiative in the broader context initiated and sponsored by members of the Community based on experiences and best practices.

Community development is a grassroots process by which communities:

- become more responsible
- organize and plan together
- develop healthy lifestyle options
- empower themselves
- reduce poverty and suffering
- create employment and economic opportunities
- achieve social, economic, cultural, and environmental goals

Community development aims to improve the quality of life—community development. Positive community development leads to mutual benefit and responsibility shared between the members of the Community. This growth is understood by its connection to capacity building and social, cultural, environmental, and economic interaction. The diversity of interests in the Community helps to build collective capacity to address issues, explore resources, find common ground, and balance competing interests. Capacity building does not only entail a deliberate and diligent effort in order to enhance the Environment (or many things).

1.7 RESEARCH GAP

I. There is no previous study to measure the impact of Corporate Social Responsibility on Community Development in the selected area.

II. No previous study is belonged to selective corporate social responsibility initiatives of business organization for minimize the social issues and improvement of natural resources in communities.

III. The analysis of effect of challenges of corporate social responsibility initiative over the community development.

1.8 RELEVANCE AND JUSTIFICATION OF THE STUDY

The current trend of globalization has made the firms realize that to compete effectively in a competitive environment, they need clearly defined business practices with a sound focus on the public interest in the markets.

1. Corporate social responsibility can be an integral element of a sustainable business. In most emerging economies, the Government must protect the interests of the public and thus gives preference to companies that take care of the interests of all the stakeholders of the company.
2. The increase in competition among the multinational companies to gain a first-mover advantage in various developing countries by establishing goodwill relationships with the Government and Society is ample testimony to this transformation.

1.9 RESEARCH QUESTIONS

A research question is an answerable inquiry of a general or specialized issue formed as the first active phase of the research process when an idea is generated. Research Questions were created to support the researcher's objectives or research effort and are then tested using Research Hypothesis. The following are the study's research questions:

RQ1. Do Corporate Social Responsibility activities of Organizations Impact variables of Community development?

RQ2. Does Business environment Variables Impact the performance of Corporate Social Responsibility activities?

RQ3. Do Challenges affect the performance of Corporate Social Responsibility activities of Business organizations?

The objectives of the Study followed these research questions.

1.10 OBJECTIVES OF THE STUDY

In terms of the study's objectives, the researcher outlines the essential study goals on which the researcher should concentrate. The researcher attempted to cover all elements of the targeted structures for this investigation. The researcher has given the following research objectives:

- To study the impact of Corporate Social Responsibility activities on different variables of Community development like youth development, Upliftment of underprivileged Communities, and nature preservation.
- To study the impact of Business environment Variables like Corporate branding, Training and development of employees, legal compliance, the policy of CSR implementation, and organization recognition on the performance of CSR activities of organizations.
- To measure the impact of business environment Challenges like political pressure, financial crisis, community pressure, etc., on Corporate Social responsibility activities of organizations.

1.11 RESEARCH HYPOTHESIS

A hypothesis is a statement that may be tested to see if it is accurate or untrue using scientific research methods or with the help of a statistical testing method. Creating a null hypothesis, which is evaluated against a specific alternative, called the research Hypothesis, is required for statistical testing of a relationship (Abramson, 1997). The research hypothesis of the study was as follows:

- **H01: There exist no significant role of Corporate social responsibility activities on community development.**
- **H02: Business Environment Variables does not significant impact on CSR activities of the organization.**
- **H03: Challenges does not impact on delivery of CSR activities in community development.**

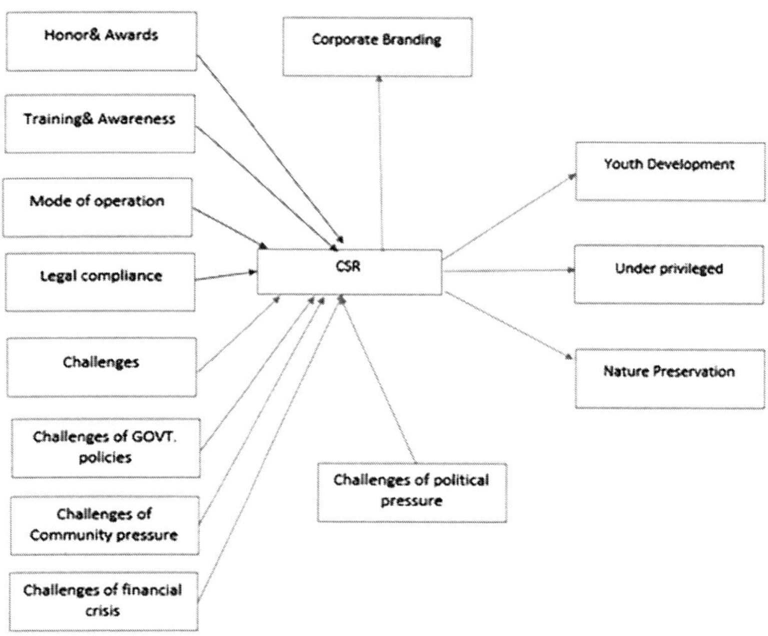

Figure 2. CSR influencing Factors
Source: Author's Compilation

Research Method & Design

The researcher must select appropriate examination procedures and appropriate methods and design to provide a framework for conducting a research project (Edwards-Dandridge, 2019). Various ideas and assumptions influence the researcher in making judgments about whether to use quantitative or qualitative research methodologies and designs in his or her research (Haneef, 2013; Johnston, 2014; Edwards-Dandridge, 2019).

Research Design: Cause and Effect Research Design will be utilized the satisfy the Objectives of the Study.

Sampling Method: A convenient sampling method will collect samples from a company representative and community members.

Sample Size: In this study sample size of 700 will be selected, and data will be collected from two Districts, each from MP & CG; in MP, the selected Districts are Annupur & Singrauli and in CG 2selected Districts are Bilaspur & Korba.

Data Collection: Primary data will be collected through interviews and questionnaires to gather information and feedback from Company representatives and community members/ beneficiaries. Secondary Information will be collected through various organizational brochures, manuals, annual reports, journals, books, magazines, etc.

Instruments: The researcher will utilize self-designed questionnaires to collect data, and the variables and items in the final instrument will be incorporated after a careful and rigorous process of questionnaire construction followed by a pilot survey for further purification of scales.

Analysis of Data

Appropriate descriptive statistical tools like arithmetic mean, standard deviation, coefficient of variation, correlation analysis, regression analysis, and t-test ANOVA will be used to interpret data.

Chapterization

The following chapters have been taken for the study.

CHAPTER 1: INTRODUCTION

CHAPTER 2: LITERATURE REVIEW

CHAPTER 3: RESEARCH METHODOLOGY

CHAPTER 4: DATA ANALYSIS & INTERPRETATION

CHAPTER5: DISCUSSION, CONCLUSION, SUGGESTIONS AND LIMITATIONS

CHAPTER- 2

Review of Related Literature

2.1 INTRODUCTION

Any research work cannot be done without an in-depth study of current research and literature, like a research paper, journal, books, and thesis. A review of literature plays a vital role in conducting a study. It provides depth knowledge about research methodology, which is used at the time of Researching because of literature review, the researcher can analyze the change of trend in that field at international and domestic levels. Knowledge of research gaps and what has been done, common lacunas of research, can be recognized through literature review. In a literature review, published research in a specific subject area was discussed, and often information was acquired in a specific field of research over a given period.

A literature review may only be a straightforward overview of the sources, but it typically has a pattern of organization that incorporates both summary and synthesis. A description is a summary of the source's vital information, but a synthesis is a reorganization of that information or a reshuffling of it. It may offer a new understanding of old content or mix old meanings with new ones. Alternatively, it could trace, including primary debates, the academic progression of the field. Furthermore, the literature review can evaluate the sources and inform the reader on the most important or relevant, depending on the situation. Reviews of literature provide you with a helpful guide to a specific topic. Literature reviews will provide an outline or serve as a steppingstone when researchers have little time to perform analysis. They are valuable reports for experts that bring them up to date on current industry trends. The scope and width of the literature review emphasize academics and the writer's reputation in his or her profession. Literature evaluations also have a good context for investigating a scholarly paper. For most research papers, detailed knowledge of the field's literature is necessary.

This chapter contains the crux of more than fifty research works related to corporate social responsibility (CSR) implementation policy, theory, Impact on community development, impact on Environment, impact on the organization, CSR representation, and how CSR was related to another field of Knowledge.

A review of related literature is collected from International and national journals, books, websites, newspapers, online blogs, etc. After reviewing existing literature, the researcher was able to find a research gap for the study; there is significantly less literature found on the study, so the researcher chose this topic.

2.2 Corporate Social Responsibility & Community Development

In this section of the literature review, the researcher includes the national and international studies related to Corporate Social responsibility and their impact on Sustainable development and different aspects of Community Development. Some Studies are as follows:

Eibiret& Parket (1973) in his analysis, 400 U.S based companies were considered and found that all the organizations were engaged in Community development activities. The researcher also considered the information of activities kinds, size of Company and included success rate and shareholders viewpoint. Findings were considered as a benchmark for planning for an already engaged program.

Low (1985) used exact figures on 80 reported companies and their annual reports es. In Singapore, to discover the standard of corporate presentation regarding CSR and Sustainable development. The researcher reported that many social disclosures were lifted in annual reports.

Guthrie and Parker (1989) conducted research based on European companies' data on CSR disclosure and their actual performance, and it was reported that CSR disclosure and CSR performance co-existence. In that way, both are influenced by each other. His research finding was considered for CSR planning by the top policymakers.

Andrew et al. (1989) used hypnotizing projections to validate the earlier Disclosures that HR is the most exposed topic taken after an item, a mass, and for a long time. Last of all, climate. In addition, the audit showed medium to far-reaching firms. It has made further social disclosures. These exposures were usually genius and not enough. Affirmation may be amassed to certify or nullify the relationship between business and industry.

Wood (1991) conducted a study of over 100 organizations that reported CSR proposes a form of obligation by corporate agreements and drills. This corporate social responsibility organizational viewpoint was expressed in the social execution of an entity, which can be assessed by how a corporation interacts with its environment, its social impact and the outcomes of its CSR approaches and activities.

E.lte (2004) conducted research to evaluate the relationship between corporate social Responsibility and Community development and the role of good governance. This study is conducted in the Niger delta, Nigeria, an underdeveloped country that eagerly needs basic infrastructure, education, health, and poverty, which is also a significant issue. So, the paper concludes that the absence of national macro-economic planning and management, enabled by fair distribution of resources and an enabling environment, has significant consequences for the overall output of global corporate (MNC) CSR initiatives in developing countries. So, we can say that if the country's economy is underperforming due to poor governance, then multinational organization contributions in the form of CSR for poverty alleviation are likely to fail to achieve the desired results. So good governance is vital to achieving the CSR goals.

Eweje(2006) Generally, multinational enterprises have a terrible reputation in the context of CSR; to examine this researcher choose oil firms in Nigeria and mining companies in South Africa for the case study. Moreover, the researcher found that there was much expectation of host communities for development programs in developing countries because they want a stable and bright future for their generation. Companies do many things for education, infrastructural development, health, and Environment, but they do not fulfill the expectation. Companies also argue that they have to pay taxes and other duties to the government, which is responsible. Community people put pressure on the Government by involving MNEs and International communities.

Idemudia (2007) Conducted research in Nigeria. He tried to examine the actual relationship between MNCs (Oil Companies) Corporate Social Responsibility and actual development of the community, and Research results indicate that the relationship between CSR and community development is much more complicated than commonly thought. In terms of the interplay of corporate motivation and policy, local culture, and structural context, the degree to which the CSR initiatives of oil MNCs have a positive or negative effect on community development is better understood.

Matten & Moon (2007) Identifies two distinct CSR components, the explicit and the implied. Explicit CSR is optional, and a company's voluntary, conscious, and sometimes deliberate intervention with specific social causes, such as supplying aid to victims of natural disasters. Implicit CSR typically consists of principles, criteria, and guidelines that arise in (compulsory and customary) conditions for organizations to tackle stakeholder problems and describe the corporate actors' ethical responsibilities in mutual rather than individual terms.

Jamali & Mirshak (2007) in a survey of businesses in Lebanon that are known for their activities, A popular trend was found to emerge, demonstrating the organic connection between an agency and the local community and the potential need for social interventions that will support Society in general and local stakeholders.

Friedman (2007) claimed that there is one and only one social isolation, a Company's commitment to use its resources and engage in events intended to gather its benefits to the degree that it remains within the quality of entertainment, which is to state, without deception or misrepresentation, engages in transparent and accessible contention.

Ismail (2009) conducted theoretical research with the help of some scholar and their work in the light of the theory of CSR and Concluded as CSR is conducted differently in different countries according to their compliance and culture. However, the results are almost the same. So, researchers suggested that CSR executives must have diversified knowledge of the different subjects and managerial skills like forecasting, planning, Controlling, and motivation; in this way, community development targets may be achieved more meaningfully.

Maon, (2009) proposed an integrative system of architecture and operation of corporate social responsibility. It consists of nine steps: corporate consciousness-raising, socially based corporate intent, precise vision, current position, strategic strategy, internal and external coordination, appraisal, and policies. She has presented the background of several case studies for this reason. Finally, for the CSR process, the analysis recognizes important success drivers.

Fisher (2009), Michael Porter, and Mark Kramer argue in the December 2006 edition of the Harvard Business Review that businesses can build socially and fiscally responsible solutions to current CSR problems by addressing corporate social responsibility

(CSR) based on corporate goals, strengths, and skills, which will provide organizational and competitive advantages. This paper discusses a case study of a Canadian SME that uses a community development system called Asset Based Community Development (ABCD) for its CSR programming. Since ABCD relies on to suggest, it provides an additional structure from which Porter and Kramer's claims can be applied to the production and preservation of social capital and can be used to achieve set goals. The ABCD system offers the means to drive CSR towards creating social change by highlighting established organizational skills and talents. CSR is the purpose, social capital is the instrument, as seen in our case study, and ABCD is the mechanism to execute the tool.

Shah & Bhaskar (2010) research study on Corporate Social Responsibility (CSR)in an Indian public sector organization, Bharat Petroleum Corporation Limited, noted that Bharat Petroleum Corporation Limited has gone beyond philanthropy and made efforts to establish local communities in conjunction with various NGOs and SHGs in order to enable them to earn their livelihoods and not to rely on any form of assistance and support from any organization. The organization's CSR programs benefit its workers and stakeholders, such as truck drivers and villagers remaining in the area. The CSR activities carried out by BPCL should be adopted by private companies and other PSUs.

Adewui et al. (2010) found that Around 46.3 percent of WAPCO 's corporate social programs were spent on responsibilities to Society, and the organization is becoming more Community-focused. Although the CSR exercises of WAPCO are directly linked to its turnover, corporate social responsibility as a turnover ratio across the study period is less than 0.5 percent. In the West African Portland Cement plc CSR budget, some categories such as health seem not to be given priority.

Hatman, (2011) in the European review of the Agriculture Economics Journal, the article 'Corporate Social Responsibility in the Food Sector' explored the value of CSR in the food sector in high-brand firms. So, businesses play an essential role in CSR.

However, small and medium-sized enterprises are less likely to meet social commitments. Furthermore, the study has shown that the food industry still strives to expand its consumer protection and dumping facilities. Consumers often favor labels or food providers that prefer CSR, offering decent goods and services.

McDonald & Lai, (2011) in an experimental analysis at Taiwan banks, it was found that customer-centered interventions impacted the mindset of banking customers towards the bank and behavioral intentions more intensely than environmental or philanthropic initiatives.

Adams's (2011) analyzed in Lebanon found no different organizations. It is handled by an ad-hoc committee of publicity, public relations, management members, and a dedicated CSR official or CSR office. I often have people coming to us wondering whether we want to sponsor them for a specific project. Moreover, we take as much of it on board as we can. Uh, we want to assist or give the deserving workers and the Society something back.

Baxi & Ray, (2012) the Aditya Birla Group has a defined emphasis on "sustainable livelihood" and "sustainable livelihood" Developed a Hub for Rural Growth and Neighborhood Projects some 12 years ago. The Center collaborated with local organizations in the villages and has devoted administrators and staff. In addition, Tata Group also has the Tata Community Development Council specially formed to implement rural development projects.

Mukharjee (2012) the new model claims that it assumes the GOI as RBI would also demonstrate its political will to mobilize its resources to advance economic inclusion. The model also assumes that complete financial inclusion, over a more extended period, contributes to sustainable profitability for RBI and commercial banks. It also hypothesized that the initiatives by central and state governments to curb poverty by various measures, Schemes, and subsidies should not cover those in need. This is required for sustainable development.

Lund-Thomsen & Pillay, (2012) A CSR analysis at oil mining sites in Nigeria showed that operation Community engagement in CSR programs strengthened the collective capacity of the neediest. However, there are few contributions to poverty eradication by enhancing essential capacity or overall health. However, most poorer people employed in fisheries or agriculture did not benefit from CSR programs in certain ventures by petroleum firms. This indicates that Community participation in construction programs can increase the potential of individuals. In addition, several developed countries have been forced both by global and local forces to participate in traditional CSR behavior in the form of industrial clusters and CSR since the late 1990s.

Prashad &Mohanty (2012) the "Sustainable Development Vis-à-vis Actual CSR" analysis was carried out. The results revealed that firms are now spending in several fields, such as child labor, groundwater, food, schooling, etc., but are not conscious of the basic needs of the poor. The study indicated that while profit earning is a natural reality for corporations, CSR is outside the company's natural and legislative obligations. The study concluded that the growth of both Community and industry in a responsible manner is sustainable development.

Pankaj et al (2012) in their article, Evolving CSR Developments in India, 30 companies from 11 sectors listed on the Bombay Stock Exchange were examined with their annual reports. Transport Machinery, Finance and Metal Processing, IT & Power, Capital Goods, Telecom, Accommodation, FMCG, Oil & Gas, Cipla, etc. were some of those industries. The study concluded that today's corporations are not only trying to make a buck but also recognizing the value of being socially friendly.

Wilson (2012) this article explores the role of social enterprises in delivering fair services to disadvantaged consumers, focusing on the vulnerability of low-income consumers to high-cost credit abuse due to lack of access to conventional financial services. It would be argued that both the state and the private sector have a role to play, through access to equal services, in providing the means through which disadvantaged consumers can resolve financial exclusion.

This cannot and should not, however, be done by increasing the provision of welfare or by relying on corporate social responsibility programmes alone. This article indicates that regulatory support for the creation and growth of social enterprises, such as community development finance institutions, can most effectively give rise to a social framework under which insecurity and insecurity are most efficient when rejecting solutions based on increased welfare or voluntary corporate social responsibility initiatives.

Nash, (2012) "CSR: contributions of Maharatna Companies of India" was analyzed and found that the commitment in the CSR region was really made by these companies. CSR investment is becoming difficult for the Indian private sector. In the coming 2012 budget, CSR allocation is more likely to be obligatory. With respect to CSR expenditures, the difference between public and private corporations will soon be reduced. In this sense, other companies who want to genuinely engage in the CSR activities of all Maharatna enterprises have the right to take the CSR activities as an ideal example and motivator.

Mzembe, (2012) different factors are found in the areas of CSR activity when it comes to behave/carry them. First of all, the areas of CSR operations that are seen to vary in the organizations can be identified according to the focus/target group. It could be contingent on the behavior of these businesses towards social problems and is primarily affected by the strong owners with essential long-term investments sustainability.

Ramana (2013) the CSR analysis was undertaken by Indian Private and Publishing Industry (Reliance Industries Ltd.) and Public Sector (ONGC), and also researched CSR Indian Government Policy and Programmes. This report examined CSR practices by select Indian private and public sector firms (CSR). The research revealed that while Indian public and private companies are making efforts in the areas of CSR, there is still a need for greater focus on CSR. The study showed that RIL and ONGC's CSR activities vary substantially because the ONGC's CSR budget is higher than RIL's during 2009-10, 2010-11, and 2011-12, and the ONGC's overall

CSR score is higher than that of RIL during 2009-10 and 2011-12.

Sharmila et al., (2013) Via a case study of the effective CSR initiative in Bukit Awang, Pasir Puteh Kelantan in Malaysia, this paper will examine the roles of government agencies in the CSR project. For this reason, a qualitative research approach examines the experiences of social players participating in the project and performs thematic data analysis. The study's outcome shows two critical functions played by the government department in the company's CSR initiative for society. The roles are as a service agent and as a group representative. These functions helped to incorporate the CSR project to improve the culture involved.

EY & Ph.D. Chambers (2013) an analysis of 50 companies' CSR operations from the S&P BSE Top 100 Index9 Analyzed to recognize the patterns in CSR in India, it was also observed that 60% of enterprises run the organization's CSR initiatives either through a particular CSR department or the Human resources department or the Corporate Communication department and 70% through NGOs.

Das (2013) the non-life insurance organizations noticed in his research Revealed far less social information than organizations for life insurance. The investigation also reveals that public life insurers have far more social data than other providers. Whereas a paired t-test shows that more social knowledge is released by private general insurance organizations as significant distinctions. In this way, the private insurance sector is more aware of community problems, so their CSR initiatives are more effective.

Vázquez (2014) paper concentrates on the regional companies that interact in their operations with both external and internal sides of CSR. To this end, the outcomes of a survey of 590 managers of corporate services have been analyzed, and the findings indicate that five variables extracted from this analysis determined the internal CSR hand. These considerations include ethical human resources strategies, the corporate sustainability culture, advancement of social programs, important pay policies, and workers' quality of life. The study findings suggest a consistent factor structure with many suitable factors. The Cronbach's alpha value derives a positive relationship with the number of 18 variables in the scale of products. To ascertain the influence of external CSR, the study proposes the theoretical and hypothetical relation between the internal and external CSR sides.

Siddiq & Javed (2014) this paper attempts to illustrate the value of CSR in enhancing organizational efficiency. The six based companies are listed in the Pakistani index. Two variables were used to analyze CSR (independent variable), and another two were evaluated organizationally (dependent variable). Primary and secondary data were used, and descriptive regression and correlation techniques were introduced for the study. The results show a very strong association between ROA and turnover, although the standard turnover deviation is also uncommon. The consequence of regression is

The suggested model does not seem necessary and appears to oppose it. Finally, some recommendations were made emphasizing the value of CSR for improving organizations' efficiency. The research is a reference for managers and a practical method for potential scientists.

Bansal & Rai, (2014) for the well-being of rural populations, most businesses conduct CSR investment, particularly around their operational areas. A potential explanation may be to create sympathy among community residents and become acquainted with the city and its needs, thus mitigating the expense of delivering services. In India, unlike developed countries where CSR operations are carried out primarily in the environmental arena, they are primarily carried out in the social sector.

Wankhade (2014) examined Indian corporations' spending on corporate social responsibility. The research further focuses on qualitative analysis of social responsibility investment of businesses in the public and private sectors as a proportion of the PAT and the disclosure sketches. The research is based on secondary knowledge obtained from the business magazine's annual reports for the 2011-12 financial year. The study showed that social responsibility investments of corporations constitute less than 2 percent of the benefit after-tax from Indian companies, although social responsibility investment and disclosure for public & private sector companies are also not substantially different. The results will help policymakers to ensure that Indian businesses raise spending on corporate social responsibility and make the Sector Responsibility Report and the Annual Report more transparent.

Chotaliya, (2014) the CSR classification and benefits were studied. This article predicted CSR awareness of the upward trend following the implementation of the Companies Act, 2013 guidelines. The paper highlights the best-driven approaches for CSR, and the main factor for applying the CSR policy was employees. Multiple ideas, therefore, as incentives for active participation in CSR activities to incentivize and reward their efforts in CSR have been prescribed.

Ramesh, (2015) attempts to study the performance of PSUs & Private Companies' CSR spending with a transparency score and recommends a few suggestions for improving the companies' CSR initiatives. Three years of data from 15 PSUs and private sector companies were gathered for the study, and CSR was compared with their respective PAT and found that public companies, Compared to private businesses, work better on CSR. The paper also suggests that, by following the guidelines, there is a need to create awareness of CSR among private sector companies. It was also suggested that CSR should be made compulsory at business schools and colleges, and universities as a subject or discipline to raise awareness of social and development issues among students.

Chhajed, (2015) tried to define CSR and CSR assessment in India. He tried to focus on how many Indian companies spend on CSR in India and around the world. He took the top 100 spending data from businesses for this purpose. And then, compared to 132 US-based businesses, they discovered that they are much ahead of Indian-based businesses. On the other hand, since the total expenditure of Indian companies was $81 million, US companies accounted for $10 billion in CSR in 2013. While he also proposed a few initiatives for both government and Indian companies to change the current scenario.

Jain, (2015) the paper seeks to understand the implications and implementation of the provisions of section 135 of the New Companies Act 2013. The paper also focuses on expenditure patterns before and after the new regulation. For this purpose, the percentage method was used to analyze the data collected from 20 companies. The allocation of CSR money was divided into four parts, and the amount was presented as a percentage. Furthermore, the same companies are again tested after the application of new legislation, and it is found that the Indian Companies Act of 2013 has brought a paradigm shift in India to corporate law and has far-reaching implications.

Ismail (2015) from the perspective of its participants in Malaysia, this study aims to examine the outcome of a Corporate Social Responsibility (CSR) program in community development. It is argued that there has been insufficient data on CSR community development, CSR providers, and CSR effects on community development in Malaysia. This research, therefore primarily explores the profiles of participants in community development CSR initiatives, the profiles of selected CSR participating companies, the orientation of corporate CSR obligations as viewed by participants, and the types of commitment of CSR participating companies to community development. By the millennium's first decade, most participating CSR companies had adopted CSR systems and had their core businesses in different sectors. The most relevant orientation was considered legal responsibility, and the minor essential orientation was ethical responsibility. The dominant type of CSR contribution was generated by activities related to education.

Chaudhari, (2016) the BSE-SENSEX-listed companies examined the exposure of CSR expenditure in their annual reports. The analysis concluded that the new CSR Act, included in the Companies-Personal Act, 2013 in Section 135, did not result in the expected results of its first year of implementation. Only 4 out of 28 companies analyzed in this study were able to spend an amount equal to the 2 percent limit of the average net profit over the last three years. He also suggested that Effective CSR can be achieved by aligning CSR activities with commercial objectives, increasing the incentive for efficient programming and implementation. It is possible only if companies implement the law on a ground basis through shared goals and government participation.

Rajendran, (2016) has attempted to explore the significant aspect of the new CSR provisions under company law 2013 and explained them. His article aims to look into and understand some of the provisions differently and clarify them from the Ministry of Enterprise (MCA). The article has notified Mr. Anil Baijal of the recommendation of the high-level committee for CSR, established by the government in February 2015. In this article, the CSR regulation sections are illustrated, the "average net profit" formula for estimating the amount for CSR, and several suggestions for solving various problems in measuring the amount of CSR.

Murali, (2017) CSR policies and activities have been studied in India and adopted by particular businesses. They also studied the investment trend of CSR businesses and concluded that a correlation occurs between the previous year's CSR expenditures and next year's PAT. To this end, 50 businesses have been taken and divided into sectors. The article focuses mainly on secondary inquiry. The text is broken into four levels. The first stage analyzes the measurement of CSR sums according to legislation and how much each organization spends. The CSR Business review of these businesses was performed at the second level. The operations on which each firm expended the CSR sum were evaluated next. Finally, the Activity-Wise sector-specific research was carried out. The findings show that the relationship between the two variables is positive and essential.

Trendfovia (2017) this paper discusses the characteristics and potential for positive community growth of Corporate Social Responsibility (CSR) sports initiatives. There is a need to fill the gap between sport-related CSR and community growth by focusing on community capacity building. While the neoliberal roots of CSR are known, the ideological varieties guiding CSR that can allow inclusiveness and cooperation in promoting group benefits must be understood.

Singh & Sarkar (2017) in their research Revolutionizing Corporate Social Responsibility in India, found that Indian organizations have been practicing CSR as part of philanthropy. There is no proper structure to execute CSR accompanied by businesses. For branding and tax advantages, most businesses conduct CSR. In its present form, corporate social responsibility is in its evolving phase. The primary priority of organizations is education, followed by the environment and water supplies.

Chung & Young (2018) analysis explores the impact of corporate social responsibility on corporate valuation, using data given by all corporations listed on the Korean exchange from 2005 to 2015. We precisely examine the relationship between corporate social transparency and corporate value with the Korea Economic Justice Institution Index, a significant indicator of corporate social responsibility in Korea. In addition, we intend to evaluate the differential features of manufacturing firms using the relationship between corporate social responsibility and firm valuation, considering the increasing exposure to the Korean manufacturing environment and the substantial impact of the global manufacturing environment. The findings strongly affirm the beneficial relationship between corporate social responsibility and corporate value. In contrast, our thorough study of the manufacturing sector reveals certain variations. The study found that corporate social responsibility as an aggressive competitive policy should be embraced by any company, considering the corporate situation.

Duca & Gherghina, (2018) the authors suggest an overview of the idea of corporate social responsibility (CSR) and emphasize its role in sustainability. As this is a term with a very brief background in the market climate of Romania, the authors provide references in this chapter to related papers in the expert literature. This chapter describes the different theoretical approaches to CSR, a general analysis of growth at the domestic and international level of CSR activities, some authors' reasons for and against the generalization of certain practices and international developments in CSR practices, and a study of Romanian CSR activities. The study's results articulate their points of view concerning the creation and associated benefits of corporate social responsibility projects in companies.

Mundakir (2018) study focused on sustainable market growth by incorporating CSR at PT. Heinz ABC Indonesia. Indonesia. By applying CSR, PT. Heinz ABC Indonesia plans to grow the organization by emphasizing environmental and social interrelationship with pollution or pollution control measures, resulting in lower costs. Developing the business using corporate responsibility in the future would therefore preserve a strong company and brand value.

Marco et al. (2018) this paper looks at the determinants and methodological interconnections between norms of transparency and environmental proactivity within a large community of businesses. With a regional emphasis reflecting the transversal cultural and socio-economic circumstances connected to the context, empirical investigations have been undertaken for 297 Aragon (Spain) companies, analyzing their environmental knowledge, efficiency, and managerial variables. The results affirm the importance of the internal factors of firms as determinants of transparency, but also the value of regional factors in the relationship of green companies with stakeholders. The positive association between duty and environmental proactivity indicates diverse methods for enforcement and participation of stakeholders.

McLennan (2019) researcher is arguing that corporate organizations only focus on CSR practices based on the perception that they never try to understand the impact of these practices on society. Researcher claim that in terms of the enormous imminent impact of the corporate presence, rather than just the deliberate CSR initiatives, societies see and analyze CSR / CCD and prioritize relationships over material performance. We outline a corporate strategy that starts with the recognition that core business activities can have a profound impact on society's long-term growth. Those successful contributions require businesses to "embrace the chaos" and cultivate the kinds of relationships that predominate.

Nwagbara & Belal (2019) paper gives insights into the negotiation experiments (persuasion theory) and the study of essential expression (CDA) in order to decode all the verbal techniques (single terms), phrases, words (clauses/sentences), an implicit but not obvious one, in a discursive manner. These language strategies (elements at a micro level), which represent more extensive social activities, complement organizational discourses (meso-elements) (macro-level elements). The authors are based on the CSR reports published by six leading Nigerian oil firms from 2009 to 2012. The results in this study indicate that Nigerian oil firms (leading Nigerian companies) use CSR reports in linguistic terms in the eyes of more prominent stakeholders, while severe complaints regarding their corporate accountability to persuade mold and portray the picture of a "responsible organization.

Hawes & Young, (2019) the popular Corporate Social Responsibility (CSR) scandals, which involve corruption, environmental degradation, IP fraud, and food protection, show that corporate social responsibility (CSR) has not yet been established in the Chinese market. One fundamental explanation is that Chinese managers consider CSR a foreign term, a series of laws placed externally, which cannot resonate with their internal views of the environment. This paper suggests a new approach to CSR based on 'vital energy (qi) that circulates through an organically interconnected normative universe (do) - an evolutionary vision of China that overcomes cultural obstacles to acceptance while building on perspectives from contemporary conduct economics and materials science at the same time. The paper offers Chinese conceptual tools for transforming a burden on companies put externally into an internally sustainable, environmentally responsible, innovative product creation.

Abdelhalim & Eldin, (2019) this paper is intended to establish a Corporate Social Development (CSR) evaluation model, which is interrelated with sustainable development, and to study the CSR case model of Egypt, to analyze whether CSR is included in the central corporate agenda. This research helps explain the CSR status in Egypt and socio-economic countries. The generalization of the evaluation outcomes in Egypt and countries with comparable situations only leads to philanthropy and little to human or business growth in most CSR experiences. The lack of a formal systemic context to coordinate the State's role in promoting CSR means that CSR cannot be related to sustainable development goals or similar strategies.

Seriki (2020) Chinese Foreign Construction Companies (CICCs) should no longer disregard the value of the construction industry in Africa since these companies hold a considerable market share in the African continent. For African economic rebirth, the building industry is of great significance, and Corporate Social Responsibility (CSR) is becoming an essential topic for developed continent business processes. In African economies, narratives surrounding the introduction of CSR in the building industry have been predominantly one-sided, considered from an international viewpoint and external anecdotes. This article, therefore, discusses CSR as a vital component of Chinese entrepreneurs' continued penetration and domination in the intensely competitive African building markets. The essay discusses how CICCs incorporate CSR, how they integrate themselves with current local and foreign peers, and the future of these businesses in Africa using CSR as a metric. For the reason and results used to recommend potential options for future CSR policymaking in local African communities where Chinese contractors are carrying out industry, citizens of the largest economy in Africa, Nigeria, who have Chinese ventures in their communities. The study revealed that CICCs were highly respected in terms of construction efficiency and appreciation of local law and customs regarding the application of CSR policy but were poor in their understanding of workers' health and environmental protection. The study shows that conservative African governments will curb the tide of rising anti-Chinese rhetoric within building on the African continent by establishing a CSR policy for all foreign contractor firms.

Amin & Lastanti (2020) the aim of this analysis is to determine, by adding Good Corporate Governance (GCG), the effect of CSR on profitability and the production of value. Corporate Social Responsibility (CSR) Calculation using the Kinder Ladenburg Domini (KLD) Social Ratings Data or Clarkson's (1995) RDAP Scale, which is an appraisal metric based on stakeholders, including environmental dimensions, commodity efficiency dimensions, community relations dimensions, diversity dimensions, and employee relations dimensions. A survey of 25 organizations with a total of 50 annual reports, financial reports, and sustainability reports was collected using the purpose-based sampling process. The findings revealed that Corporate Social Responsibility (CSR) has a favorable and vital impact on profitability yet did not affect the development of value, and the effect of Corporate Social Responsibility (CSR) on profitability was not mediated by Good Corporate Governance (GCG) but was able to mediate the influence of Corporate Social Responsibility (CSR) on value creation.

Aprianti &Reonald (2020) the paper is focused on developing a framework for examining the influence of the Corporate Social Obligation of The Body Shop Indonesia on various marketing actions, including Cause Relevant Marketing, through different suggestions based on the context and effects of business and social actions in society. The influence of this behavior is associated with three dimensions of marketing performance: economic and social interventions. The findings of this analysis show that the corporate social responsibility of The Body Shop Indonesia complies with the laws of corporate social responsibility of corporations in Indonesia.

Demirel (2020) this paper is intended to examine the interaction between the sponsorship and socially conscious views of the customer of professional sports teams. More precisely, this analysis examines whether sponsorship of professional sports teams causes buyers to view a sponsoring brand as socially conscious and what factors can create expectations of CSR and eventual consumer reaction. The longitudinal research findings show that professional sports team brand sponsorship adds to the socially conscious reputation of this brand and that sponsorship fit induces a sponsoring brand's CSR impressions by customers. The field trial findings also established CSR expectations as a mechanism that drives sponsorship's impact on customer conduct against a sponsorship brand. Finally, the task of team naming was seen to shape the sponsorship's impact as a borderline disease.

2.3 CSR& ENVIRONMENT

In this section of the literature review, the researcher includes the national and international studies related to Corporate Social responsibility and their impact on environmental factors and different aspects of Community Development. Some Studies are as follows:

Savage (1994) stated that about 50 of the 115 South African companies. Percentage of businesses make social disclosures of human resources (89 percent). As the central theme. Disclosure of human capital linked to pay, working practices, pay, and proportionate open entrances. Some social leaks consolidate aggregates Commitment (72 percent) and exposure to the environment (63 percent).

Dim et al. (1996) attempted to clear up the divulgence of social and natural data in the yearly reports of vast organizations by reference to perceptible attributes of those organizations. A broad arrangement has endeavored to be set up regardless of whether segments, for example, corporate size, preferred position, and industry pieces, can enlighten organizations' disclosure rehearses—the outcomes from these studies fabulously. North American and Australasian pieces are, taking everything into account, uncertain. This Paper has given an augmentation of forming by considering a more disaggregated detail of social and typical introduction and utilizing a point-by-point time course of activity informational collection. Like this, the paper endeavored two potential explanations for the shakiness of earlier exploration: explicitly that any relationship between corporate characteristics furthermore, presentation is needy upon the sort of revelation and that any such affiliations are not suffering through time industry.

Tsang (1998) completed a longitudinal survey of currency, sustenance, refreshments, and motel efforts from 1986 to 1995, said that of the 33. Just 17 businesses have revealed information on corporate social news. Topical Style Focus research demonstrated that the most uncovered topic is HR, trailed by gathering Integration, and the climate, among others. The speculation on validity has been pronounced as Clarification of corporate social news. Attached the separation measurements were. It was guided to see if there was any qualification between the three organizations. At an elementary level, businesses are yet to show less environmental knowledge than lodgings. Exposures of the other two undertakings were not essential; it was unmistakable.

Jones (2005) contended that rehashed-related organizations on the basis that the benefits for such actions are high, exchanges with partners based on confidence and cooperation are encouraged to be transparent, efficient, and moral. In addition, institutional methodologies were used in his study to test environmental, social responsibility.

Husain et al. (2006) in corporate annual reports, 'Corporate Social and Environmental Disclosure in Developed Countries: Confirm from Ban Jubilantesh' broke down the degree and extent of social and biological reporting. A presentation record was created and used to calculate the degree of introduction rendered by firms in annual accounts. This research revealed significant gaps in racial and social classes.

Environmental disclosure, as calculated by average social and environmental projections In Ban Jubilantesh, the natural disclosure list. In the same way, the audit reported that not many Ban Jubilantesh businesses were attempting to include social and biological data on an unshakable preface, which was often subjective. Companies in BanJubilantesh tended to have the lowest rate of social and environmental transparency.

Ghosh (2014) tried to find out the the private sector's contribution to community development and notes that the firms have been taking responsibility for Educational, environmental issues, rural development and health problem, empowerment, drinking water and sanitation, and peripheral development. Manufacturing and service sector companies have taken commendable measures toward education and healthcare. We aid and assist the government in adopting policies to strengthen society.

Verma& Kumar (2014) conducted research and tried to find out the CSR spending pattern. The emphasis was on CSR spending by businesses. For thirty companies listed in the BSE Sensex, the research was completed. The result indicates that under each of the three heads under which corporate social responsibility spending is categorized in this research, several organizations do not have any allocations. Throughout the report, spending on emissions and environmental control initiatives was only conducted by one organization. None of the organizations spent 2% of their income on CSR exercises during the whole period of study. The average CSR expenditure is less than a percent as a benefit percentage, suggesting that organizations Under this head of expenditure are not inclined toward spending. Therefore, the study concludes that compulsory spending of two percent of the income on CSR exercises is justified to some degree by looking at the past CSR spending of blue-chip organizations.

2.4 CSR &HUMAN RESOURCES

The literature review on human resources regarding Corporate Social responsibility includes the national and international studies related to the impact and issues of Human Resources and different aspects of Community Development. Some Studies are as follows:

Kilcullen and Koolstra (1999) based on changing the part of corporate ethics, and that is CSR. They found that CSR had taken hold as an advance and, however, as an advance. A few associates still esteem exploitative lead regardless, and several more companies. Accept the social responsibility of their accomplices.

Protohuman et al. (2000) Corporate Social News in Singapore, covers five subjects: the environment, HR, necessity, determination, and stuff and organizations to organize. Auditing is completed by demonstrating the relationship between the scale of the organization and the CSRD. It is that the partnership was questionable with regards to business and corporate social news. Financially better-performing companies have been seen to be more arranged for Company Social Reporting. It also attested to the way HR was the most exposed topic, and the respect was taken from winning firms after further corporate social reporting is Sharpening.

Sunee et al. (2006) the 40 largest Thai corporations were examined to examine the meaning and nature of social news for companies. On five main topics, corporate social reporting transparency was assessed. To explain the degree of transparency, the number of terms and the example examination were used. A reason for the market scale of the Spearman Rank association was used to relate to the corporate social offering. The survey reported that 37 to 42 percent of the overall corporate social introduction was the most revealed range for HR subjects. It was accompanied by a meeting that first extended and then diminished. The climate and objects that declined in sensitivity over time were in third place. Of these 40 Thai firms, imperatively was the scarcest point disclosed.

Sweeney (2009) in a Shell Australia sample, employees have been identified

CSR volunteering impacts their mood favorably. In contrast to non-velocitator, these workers are more optimistic about colleagues, and more Job efforts are as planned. A positive relation between CSR was noted and a company's potential to recruit, inspire and retain workers.

Bhattacharya & Sen (2010) employee volunteering has been addressed as a form of corporate social responsibility by organizations that include more permanent staff in corporate voluntary programs. It offsets the harmful working properties. The lack of understanding among domestic and foreign stakeholders prohibits an organization from benefiting from strategic CSR operations.

TUZCU (2014) the paper explores the understanding of corporate social responsibility workers and examines their perception's effects on workplace participation and work satisfaction. For this reason, TUPRAS oil refinery workers were used as a sample population where 864 people were employed, and the perception was used for the study of 104 staff from the five-point Likert scale standardized questionnaire. Exploratory component analysis was used to investigate the dimensionality. In addition, the chi-square test, t-test, and ANOVA were used for further analysis. An irrelevant association between corporate engagement and job satisfaction, and CSR perception was discovered in the study. In addition, the paper proposed that the credibility of an organization can be enhanced by accelerating CSR, particularly from the perspective of its employees and stakeholder

Palaniammal (2016) the study sheds light on employees' view of CSR and its effect on the attitude and level of employees of awareness and the way of supporting CSR practices in the leather industry. A detailed analysis of 125 samples obtained from NAG Yang Shoes (P) Ltd. was used for this purpose. After a study, it was found that corporate social responsibility has beneficial effects on the mindset, efficiency, dedication to the market, and the degree of happiness of employees. Only then will the organizations in the CSR sector succeed in volunteerism and growth. In addition, the organization and government could impart employees' perceptions, skills, and business words,' which would help them improve their abilities because most leather industry workers are not well-educated.

2.5 CSR REPORTING

In this section of the literature, the review researcher includes the national and international studies related to Corporate Social responsibility and their impact and issues of reporting. Some Studies are as follows:

Jeffery and Unerman (2000) consideration of the records that should be reviewed for organizational social monitoring and techniques used for quantum estimation Corporate Social Knowledge. They advised that the surveys were focused solely on the substance. Analysis of annual accounts would prove to be utterly incomplete and beguiling. Image of corporate social news with a wide variety of details on this On Socioeconomic Problems Documents rather than periodic accounts existed, and there were daily undertakings. Concerning the survey's assessment technique shows that the use of sentences for the calculation of the in comparison to terms or grades of pages, the amount of CSD will ensure more critical Accuracy at the expense of reducing the essence of analysis.

Belal (2001) pointed to the non-appearance of relevant corporate research disclosures of social responsibility that have been made concerning governments. In this survey In Ban Jubilates, the findings of an overview of CSR experience were published. Despite that, using content analysis tests the degree and number of exposures, The socio-political and money-related environment in which these exposures were analyzed

Richardson et al. (2002) between 1992 and 1996, it was reported that more than their social and routine implementation had been recorded by 1000 corporations worldwide. Exposures were made to the degree of documents covering annual accounts, available reports, open data, Proclaims and progresses. As of late, there are apparently noticeable instances of Stand-alone reports on socially competent activities are published.

Tune (2002) coordinated gatherings of seven generous MNCs in the compound and the United Kingdom and Germany's medicinal portions to interpret something substantial inside Components that form the level and essence of social news for companies. The Country of the Origination of the corporate scale reporting and reporting process and impact of corporate culture Critical Management.

Tune (2002) led a relevant review of Alpha's business to present the 'reporting-execution' snapshot cleft. By examining the content of the numerous annual reports, it was reported that the reports did not discuss the educational needs of various accomplices on reasonable, social, and environmental concerns. The author suggested obligatory monitoring and survey laws and a progressive update of the organizational structure.

Cowen et al. (2004) researched the essence and recurrence of corporate social Obligatory disclosures, their situations and designs, and their general associations with corporate size and profitability. This survey hoped to extend the current learning of the interaction between various organizational features and particular forms of disclosure of social responsibilities in the light of a wide variety of U.S. corporate annual reports. Corporate size and sector characterization were correlated with specific forms of exposure, whereas the proximity of the Corporate Social Responsibility Advisory Committee tended to be interfaced with a particular form of launch.

Nongnooch and Sherer (2004) concluded their investigation into Thai corporate social reporting activities and insistently found that Thai practices were not prepared to recognize their full potential to fill in as stimulating communications. The creators have thrown fine details to the conductors about the staff's exceptional and loathsome working conditions. A marginal decrease in the number of businesses reporting social and regular details from 86 percent in 1993 to 77 per penny in 1993.

Samuel (2004) in the test testing, discovered that a growing number of companies In the United Kingdom are evident from their size that corporate social news is advantageous to them. Thus, 80 percent of FTSE (Financial Times Stock Exchange)-100 businesses have information, in some cases, about their daily execution, social effects, or both. In comparison, reporting sharpens from a great degree of mind-boggling and processes handled all around to a short say in the companies' annual accounts. One of the impressive discoveries was that by suggesting different courses of action for the presentation of corporate social knowledge, the couple of global and neighbourhood affiliations counteract rather than propel the reason behind social reporting.

Ki-Hoon (2007) the study concluded that most industries in South Korea are to consider the noticeability of partnerships with main accomplices in the electronic industry. The use of extensive auditable criteria for external responsiveness has been denied. The study was accomplished using an explorative arrangement by driving open end and through meetings. Subjective data was collected on top management tasks, implementation, and reporting of social and climate, fines and disciplines, and finally, eco things. The packaging analysis was carried out to verify bunches such as loafer, limbo, champion, and fire warrior on the adoption of corporate social responsiveness.

Nazli (2007) the effects of ownership arrangement on corporate social systems were studied by Nazli (2007). In Malaysian business annual accounts, the duty introduction (CARs). The survey used a Plan for the presentation of CSR to determine the extent of CSR disclosure in annual reports and an Alternate backslide research to break down proprietorship partnership's structure and CSR transparency standards in annual reports. It has been known that also There is an impressive improvement among the most extensive and properly traded stocks in Malaysia; Revealed in corporate annual reports in the calculation of social events. Because of distinct backslide examinations, culmination shows that unfaltering of targets, Companies in the boss holds a higher level of substantial valuation shares (supervised by the owner). Companies reported less CSR knowledge at an elementary stage, whereas companies in on a straightforward basis, the company was a centrist shareholder who discovered more in their yearly accounts, CSR details.

Barut (2007) in his proposal, the success and degree of the primary 100 stubborn social news by (TBL) Triple Bottom Line report Australia Businesses to assess the degree of corporate liability for TBL news, the Global Monitoring Operation (GRI Sustainability Reporting Guidelines, 2002) data structure has been used as a benchmark for exposures and as a model After that, to allow this determination of the content of the disclosures. It was based on the studies' financial, popular, and social fragments. The declarations were made Skewed against the climate, but social exposures were evident and broadened over time.

2.6 ISSUES OF CSR

In this literature section, the review researcher includes the national and international studies related to Corporate Social responsibility and its issues. Some Studies are as follows:

Imam (2002) in a correct analysis, it was found that by far, most of the reported companies in Ban Jubilantesh did not have any information about the country, HR, social affairs, Order, and in 1996-97, consumers. However, some competitive businesses have disclosed some Relevant knowledge; it was in no circumstances adequate in discharging social details obligations. In a correct analysis, it was found that most of the reported Companies in Ban Jubilantesh did not have any information about the country, HR, social affairs, Order, and in 1996-97, consumers. However, some competitive businesses have disclosed some Relevant knowledge; it was in no circumstances adequate in discharging social details obligations. Any details collected by these businesses are subjective in terms of Nature, and the introduction quality is substantially low. Be that as it might, HR, much of it by far, the essence of the news was contextual. Many businesses overlook alternate views, such as the environment, consumers, assemble concerns, and other social views.

Garcia-Ayuso and Larrinaga (2003) that size had been hypothesized by observational research; the company's benefit and future environmental effects are the essential components that illuminate A calculation of uncovered knowledge. The biological effects of the operations Moreover, these firms tend to get more thought from print media once they are done. The findings also revealed that two variables are correlated explicitly with the measure of common the possible average effect of the organization and the level of knowledge exposed are the associations' media spectrum. It was discovered that approximately 13 percent of the objects were regularly discovered in the record, about details. The effects of the backslide study perceived scale, performance, and risk to be related to the presentation of knowledge on social responsibility in a general context and unambiguously.

Harvard Business Review on Corporate Responsibility (2003) it is one of the Circulated Harvard Business School Press book game plans. It is a series of papers on Corporate social responsibility and unique parts of philanthropy that consider the structure of discovering the landing on corporate Accountability and the process for Kosei took after by Canon. The book is likely to be written on numerous new issues related to the congruity of liberality and ethics and industry, but no paper has spoken about the need, the introduction section, and examples of corporate social discoveries.

Song and Zutshi (2004) investigated the drivers that drive the business world. They continued to discuss group exercises. They were watching the two main drivers That push businesses to behave in a socially tested and proven manner. They were represented to be moral side interest towards each one of the accomplices, not simply to the shareholders and broadening the statement that they were able to go on energy to offer insights about social, general, and exemplary problems. It was believed that corporate social news could minimize the costs of budgetary liability by keeping together and enhancing the corporate reputation with the public, journalists, state powers, and buyers.

Ice et al. (2005) it was reported that discrete accounts, out of regular annual reports, The first corporate platform is the least imperative source of corporate social exposure knowledge and expected that additional a la mode and less traditional sensitivity reports would replace them. Discrete reports provide the most of the However, frustratingly, it was controlled by traditional disclosures, a rough indicator of social appearance. Inconsistencies and radical clefts have limited the convenience of discrete studies. However, considering the locations offered a wider variety of exposures, the ultimate dependence on these reports was undoubtedly not predicted or suggested.

Song et al. (2008) assumed that the exercises of CSR would provoke first movement Advantage because it was vital to the focal purpose of the affiliation, linked to the firm's Relevant points of interest, and most importantly, where external points of interest have been made accessible Spectator gatherings. The resource-based perspective and asymmetry of the producer used the Approach of first-mover inclinations to the declaration of their investigation.

Mirfazli (2008) inspected Corporate Responsibility Information Grouping Disclosure as found in annual reports of critical and produced endeavors Clusters, guy. Annual reviews became penniless around the use of the material examination system. The results have shown that the main social introduction of the selected companies Indonesia Stock Exchange was the focus of job (51.60 percent) followed by the client. Theme (19.40%), the topic of culture (14.70%), and the universal point (14.30%) Percent, independently. In comparison, it was observed that there were no substantial differences in the presentation of the number of social disclosures in all subjects assembled between firms in the simple and synthetic classes of enterprises or the variety of enterprises.

Lin (2009) between 2002 and 2004, 1000 Taiwanese cases were investigated in which companies included their R&D spending as one of their corporate plans for sustainable development; their charitable expenditure was also defined as CSR donations. A positive association between CSR and financial results was established based on theoretical assertions and observational data in the literature. When properly defined, they find that while CSR does not have a substantial positive effect on short-term financial results, it does provide a surprising long-term fiscal benefit.

Chen (2012) paper discussed the fundamental concept of the applicability of SPSS 17.0 edition factor analysis. Thermal power firms were used for this purpose as the research population. The study showed that all thermal power industries' social efficiency was insufficient to have a substantial effect of CSR on samples. In addition, thermal power companies had to stress every part of their management and control but had terrible relationships with external stakeholders.

Sobhani et al. (2009) said that the various partners of the BanJubilantesh firms are constantly being specifically aware of the company's activities.

The Securities and Exchange Commission (SEC), the regulatory body for stock trading, has made a fundamental move to set up the corporate governance of the listed firms in BanJubilantesh. The scientists have sought to return to the status of CSED by material review. Annual reports from 100 firms on both the Dhaka Stock Trade and the Chittagong Stock Exchange have shown that exposure has risen over the last ten years.

Azim et al. (2009) researchers analyzed registered companies' corporate social reporting and found that there is a significantly less proportion of companies willing to divulge corporate social reporting, and most of the companies showed significantly less information about corporate responsibilities. The researcher also found that money-saving companies secured a higher rank regarding CSRD.

Pratten and Mashat (2009) research in Libya found that there was a vibrant change in CSR from the west. Because Libya is an Islamic country, and its government agenda was more influenced by communist ideology, the social responsibility operation and reporting model of that also changed from the rest of the world.

Ehsan &Ahmed (2012) the viewpoint of Pakistan is essential. They found that the social obligation of the organization's healthy behavior strengthens the trust of the organization's workers and gives them motivation, and shapes their self-confidence. They also explore the meaning of the relationship between employees and corporate social responsibility in Pakistan's situations, using data from about one hundred industrial companies for the period 2006-2009. To study the results, the investigator used applied statistical methods and techniques focused on Correlation and Generalized

Least Square Random Effect Regression. The study results showed that, in Pakistan's manufacturers, the essence of the employee-CSR affiliation is optimistic. The positive affiliation thus stresses the optimistic social actions in the manufacturing sector of organizations in Pakistan.

Lompo & Francois (2013) conducted research in the Nigeria delta del Nigeria and found that there were two types of companies regarding corporate social responsibility, and their impact on society also differs. One of them fallowed top to bottom approach had less impact, and another type of company had more impact than the bottom-to-top approach; this research revealed that more participation impacted more.

N Guruvaiah (2013) explores the measurability of the effect on company results of corporate social responsibility. The paper has elaborated on CSR as a younger pattern of saving money to uplift society for a higher quality product. The essential data were obtained by standardized questionnaire and secondary from the business website for this analysis from the press, staff, and customers relating to the CSR activities. For the 300-sample size, random sampling techniques are used. In the study, 62% of industrial businesses focus on environmental CSR problems. In comparison, 72% of support agencies depend on social problems while their operations do not significantly affect the community.

Hornungova, (2014) by using multidimensional statistical approach factor analysis, the article describes social success variables. For this reason, a survey analysis was carried out using 250 workers from 32 organizations in the information and communication operations field. Three variables were defined based on the paper, one belonging to the environment and two others belonging to social influences. Companies were also recommended to define important success metrics and to consider how these indicators should be integrated into organizational management to facilitate sustainable reporting.

2.7 CSR AND CORPORATE BRANDING

Margolis J. D., (2007) through performing Meta-Analysis, Corporate Social Performance (CSP) and Corporate Financial Performance (CFP) were analyzed. The net influence was positive but limited. Going further, they explored those implications across nine CSP groups. They observed that the correlation is most significant for evaluating the fundamental aspects of charitable donations, exposed misdeeds, and environmental performance, and when CSP was measured more generally by self-reported observational impressions and social performance. The organization was weakest for the precise dimensions of

CSP was analyzed more generally by corporate practices and accountability and when by third-party evaluations and mutual fund screens. While the findings indicated no financial penalty for CSP, they imply at least as clear a correlation from previous CFP to subsequent CSP as the reverse. They concluded that a set of minimum requirements should be followed if future research on the relation continues. Ideally, however, attempts to identify a connection should be redirected to explain better why businesses are following CSP, the processes linking prior CFP to subsequent CSP, and how businesses are handling the task of concurrently pursuing both CSP and CFP.

Malik (2014), CSR's effect on the financial results of banks in Pakistan's service sector is the crucial subject of the report. The study gathers data from 2008 to 2012 from the banks' annual reports. The quantity used by the banks in CSR as an independent variable was calculated to validate the relationship between CSR and financial return analyzes. To assess financial efficiency, they were taken as dependent variables. The outcome indicated a favorable relationship between CSR and the banks' financial results.

Chetty et al. (2015) the relationship between CSR and CFP were investigated for ten years from 2004 to 2013. The research measured the short-term effect of CSR on the financial returns of businesses participating in the Socially Responsible Investment

Index of the Johannesburg Securities Exchange. The CFP data was gathered from the McGregor BFA database and calculated using accounting-and-market dependent metrics. The Ordinary Least Squares (OLS) approach has been used as a statistical instrument to analyze the impact of CSR on CFP in the long term. The result indicated a significant positive interaction between CSR companies highlighting their financial performance, strengthening customer relationships, and more productive management.

Awan (2015) the paper's focus was primarily on the effect of CSR on the Ghee and Fertilizer industries' financial output of companies in Southern Punjab, Pakistan. It was an exploratory analysis to discover the effect of independent variables (CSR) on dependent variables (financial performance). In order to assess the attitude of the selected businesses towards CSR, primary data were collected through the standardized questionnaire with a five-point Likert scale, and secondary data were also collected through annual reports of selected firms. The key aim of the analysis was to examine the conditions in which social justice impacts the financial performance of businesses. The research focused on the conditions in which social responsibility positively impacts corporate financial performance. The findings were obtained from several points of view, such as socioeconomic, environment-focused, employee-orientated, business CSR and the fact that CSR has positively contributed to an improvement in revenue and capital returns of the firms. Finally, the paper concluded that businesses heavily engaged in CSR achieve a higher image, better profits, and increased performance in addition to consumer loyalty.

Ghosh (2017) the influence of Corporate Social Responsibility (CSR) on financial results has been studied. They analyzed 2011 to 2015 on 36 firms listed on the London Stock Exchange (LSE). CSR was used as an independent variable, and Return on Assets (ROA) and Return on Equity (ROE) were used as dependent variables for this purpose. Convenience sampling was used as a sampling method. They used a positive model as an optimistic approach, and objective evidence was used for the analysis. The study followed the explanatory research design, and secondary data was gathered and analysis using E-views tools was carried out. To research the regression of impacts and AS a statist, descriptive statistics were included. They used four factors to research CSR: corporate donation, protection of workers, elimination of greenhouse gas emissions, and waste reduction. The results indicate that after review, corporate giving, workforce protection and waste control do not have a big effect on financial success.

Nevertheless, reducing greenhouse gas emissions has a relevant but detrimental effect on financial results. The study concluded that reducing greenhouse emissions raises the equity of the ROA and shareholders. The researcher also indicated that Tobin's Q or stock return might be used over an extended period to get a more solid conclusion for calculating long-term financial success metrics.

Bafna (2017) using annual reports from 2014 to 2016 in India, the paper discusses the effect of CSR on the company's financial performance. The relationship between CSR and CFP and its influence on variables has been found using correlation analysis and regression analysis. The findings found that CSR substantially positively affects the company's net income but has no significant impact on the firm's EPS and ROA.

Zameer (2018) the association between CSR and financial results has been studied in the Indian sense. Secondary data was obtained from 28 Indian trading firms listed on the Bombay Stock Exchange (BSE) for the 10-year period from 2007 to 16. Content analysis was used for the study to draw CSR data from annual reports, and 1 and 0 scales were used to demonstrate the presence or absence of items to generate one CSR score. Profitability and stock market return success metrics were used as dependent variables, and the company's size, the company, the age of the company, risk, and capital intensity were used as control variables to evaluate the effect. The regression model was used as the statistical tool to study the relationship between CSR-profitability and CSR-market measures. In addition, the method of factor analysis has also been used to construct a composite index. The KMO value of the sampling adequacy is 0.69, and the Bartlett Sphericity Test has also been found suitable. The study used the robust standard error model to produce the best linear unbiased estimator for results. The paper concludes that initiatives on social responsibility can be seen as a strategy that creates legitimacy, reputation, and competitive advantages.

2.8 CHALLENGES OF CSR

Druker (1984) the importance of corporate social responsibility defines the social obligation is to confirm or distribute, the businessman's initiative duty as for the community of society, the responsibility for social effects is the duty of an administration not on the ground that it is a social duty, but rather because it is a business duty.

In their survey, **Douglas and Christopher (1999)** highlighted the need for Characteristic news requirements to be carried out without baffling likeness and to be reviewed by outsiders. Reliability of social activities. Daily records in written duplicates and on. The grounds were kindly distinct.

Tune (2002) led a relevant review of Alpha's business to present the 'reporting-execution' snapshot cleft. By examining the content of the numerous annual reports, it was reported that the reports did not discuss the educational needs of various accomplices on reasonable, social, and environmental concerns. The author suggested obligatory monitoring and survey laws and a progressive update of the organizational structure.

Newell (2005) researcher tries to find out the relation between private sector organization's CSR initiatives and community expectation and their accountability; this research is conducted in the context of India, but worldwide literature is used as a supporting document, and research was concluded as accountability of corporate organization towards the society due legal compliance, but many factors make hurdle for effective CSR initiative like political pressure, social pressure, monetary factors and some rule

&regulation of the state. Researchers indicate that accountability in every sphere of society can increase the effectiveness of the Corporate Social Responsibility Initiative.

Atale & Helge (2014) in his report, it was revealed that public sector organizations have been in the early stages voluntarily introduced CSR operations. As the operation was voluntary, these services are run by organizations according to company guidelines. Organizations face difficulties meeting the required CSR mandate following the implementation of compulsory CSR policies by the Department of Public Enterprise (DPE). The DPE should implement the proposed structure to track CSR initiatives efficiently.

Tiwari (2014) conducted research titled: A case study on NTPC Vindhya Nagar, Singrauli (M.P) India" and found that NTPC Vindhya Nagar Singrauli 's CSR arrangements are not adequate. Questionnaires were used by different members and individuals of neighboring villages. The scoring was based on a five-point scale, and the percentage score was rearranged according to the formula. The result shows that the n scoring was based on five-point scale, and the score was rearranged according to the formula.

Mundra (2016) highlighted situations where complying with CSR would be a problem for firms and the best ways to overcome these difficulties. In addition, the report refers to some aspects of corporate section 135 of the 2013 CSR read rules (CSR policy) 2014 on granulated accounting, auditing, and compliance. A close-up review of firms' existing accounting, auditing, and regulatory practices, recognizing the latest CSR profit from CSR activities over the three financial years directly preceding them. Moreover, he sought, in settling on the amount allotted for CSR operations, to face up to the problems of various types of businesses. The paper focuses solely on CSR investment, accounting, regulation, and the problems firms face in allocating CSR spending.

Kapoor & Dhamija (2017) in his research, he noted that Indian organizations had attempted to fulfill the mandatory CSR spending criteria. Collectively, 74% of the mandated amount was spent by organizations, and over two-thirds of the organizations in the study spent more than 75% of the mandated amount on CSR exercises. Multi-National corporations have done slightly better than divisions of the public sector and other private sector organizations.

Tsene & Briana, (2019) a new generation of socially conscious companies have arisen that focuses on shared ideals and social effects. In this case, the authors regard common morality as the fundamental component of the current social responsibility edition. Can innovative CSR methods successfully handle the most harmful effects of a crisis as the lack of faith and prestige, and rebuild the image of a business by multiple positive impacts? Lidl Hellas revealed the label apotalidl just before Christmas 2017, a digital campaign that has a social impact. Any digital use of the sentence shall buy for the needy ten meals. Ten meals. Here we see an entire sideline to every appreciation problem that concentrates on long-term social impact.

4.9 CHAPTER SUMMARY

Based on available literature & content, the researcher tries to get insights into Corporate Social Responsibility activities and their different aspects, like CSR and Corporate branding, Issues of CSR, and Challenges of CSR. Also, analyze the role of CSR in Community Development. The literature review was essential to find the research gap, the selection of objectives, and the construction of the hypothesis.

CHAPTER- 3

Research Methodology

3.1 INTRODUCTION

This chapter was related to the 'Research Methodology 'of the present study. Which covered all aspects of conducting research like methods of analyzing theoretical model, designing the research question, identifying objectives, methods construct of the tool, selecting a research method, selection population and sample, procedure of data collection and data cleaning, analyzing data, testing of hypothesis and interpreting the results of the study.

3.2 RESEARCH QUESTIONS

A research question is an answerable inquiry of a general or specialized issue formed as the first active phase of the research process when an idea is generated. Research Questions were created to support the researcher's objectives or research effort and are then tested using Research Hypothesis. The following are the study's research questions:

RQ1. Do Corporate Social Responsibility activities of Organizations Impact variables of Community development?

RQ2.Does Business environment Variables Impact the performance of Corporate Social Responsibility activities?

RQ3. Do Challenges affect the performance of Corporate Social Responsibility activities of the Business organization?

The objectives of the Study followed these research questions.

3.3 OBJECTIVES OF THE STUDY

In terms of the study's objectives, the researcher outlines the most crucial study goals on which the researcher should concentrate. The researcher attempted to cover all elements of the targeted structures for this investigation. The researcher has given the following research objectives:

- Study the impact of Corporate Social Responsibility activities on different variables of Community development like youth development, Upliftment of underprivileged communities, and nature preservation.
- To study the impact of Business environment Variables like Corporate branding, Training and development of employees, legal compliance, the policy of CSR implementation, and organization recognition on the performance of CSR activities of organizations.
- To measure the impact of business environment Challenges like political pressure, financial crisis, and community pressure on Corporate Social responsibility activities of organizations.

3.4 RESEARCH HYPOTHESIS

A hypothesis is a statement that may be tested to see if it is accurate or untrue using scientific research methods or with the help of a statistical testing method. Creating a null hypothesis, which is evaluated against a specific alternative, called the research Hypothesis, is required for statistical testing of a relationship (Abramson, 1997). The research hypothesis of the study was as follows:

- H01: There exists no significant role of Corporate Social Responsibility activities on community development.
- H02: Business Environment Variables do not significantly impact the organization's CSR activities.
- H03: Challenges do not impact on the delivery of CSR activities in community development.

3.5 RESEARCH METHOD & DESIGN

The researcher must select appropriate examination procedures and appropriate methods and design to provide a framework for conducting a research project (Edwards-Dandridge, 2019). Various ideas and assumptions influence the researcher in making judgments about whether to use quantitative or qualitative research methodologies and designs in his or her research (Haneef, 2013; Johnston, 2014; Edwards-Dandridge, 2019).

3.5.1. Researcrh Methods

This study was quantitative, and the goal of this research was to analyze whether factors of community development were influenced by CSR activities and factors of the business environment like corporate branding, Training, and development of employees, legal compliance, the policy of CSR implementation, and recognition of organization predicting CSR activities according to the conceptual model of the Study in particular contest Community Development. Quantitative analysis was based on statistics, which is used to examine the suggested model by assessing the hypotheses that reflect the relationship between pre-determined variables, allowing for the generalization and formulation of predictions from an extensive sample data set (Haneef, 2013; Edwards-Dandridge, 2019). Quantitative research also incorporates an unbiased and positivist method, which comprises testing hypotheses with the help of numerical data sets and statistical techniques, as well as the concept of rational thinking, which is devoid of any data manipulation (Haneef, 2013; Karlsen & Larrea, 2014; Poortman & Schildkamp, 2012; Edwards-Dandridge, 2019). Quantitative research, on the other hand, involves a systematic and detailed analysis of the relationships between several but distinct variables or constructs (Onen, 2016). Quantitative research design offers more ways to collect data and assess the constructs or variables of populations to generalize the results toward the actual population (Apuke, 2017). Even though mixed research methodology and qualitative research designs both have advantages. The researcher used quantitative methodologies to obtain results, and the data gathered can be analyzed for a whole population.

3.5.2 Research Design

The researcher used a non-experimental 'quantitative research design for this study.' In their study, Martin and Bridgmon (2012) identified three types of quantitative research designs:

- Research designs based on correlations
- Experimental research designs."
- Quasi-experimental research designs.

The correlational design is used in research studies to collect data from respondents without altering or manipulating the respondents' condition or surroundings. Statistical tests are also utilized to assess and interpret the outcomes derived from the data set (Asamoah, 2014). Thus, a correlational research design was used for the current quantitative research. Which firmly executes and shows whether factors of the Business environment like corporate branding, honors and awards, implementation policy of CSR, training of employees, legal compliance, and factors of community development like Youth development, preservation of nature, and upliftment of the underprivileged community and CSR activities of Corporate social responsibility was mutually correlated or not. Martin & Bridgmon (2012) used an experimental research strategy in which they exercised cause-effect associations on structure and supports (done through manipulated efforts) on certain constructs or factors to regulate their effect on associated measures and outcomes. Experimental and correlational study designs are two different techniques for achieving predictability among the variables or constructs' relationships. Randomized usage and mechanized sets are included in experimental research designs; however, randomized control sets are not included in correlational study designs. As a result, the experimental research design does not meet the goals of the current study. In assessing the frequent link between variables or constructs, quasi-experimental research design differs from correlational research design. Quantitative researchers frequently employ and apply quasi-experimental research designs to observe causal relationships between variables or constructs by comparing many treatments (Zellmer-Bruhn et al., 2016; Edwards-Dandridge, 2019). Quantitative researchers frequently use correlational researcher design to examine the prevalent relationship between variables. It also aids in determining the degree of "correlation" between variables or conceptions by separating independent and dependent variables (Inabinett & Ballaro, 2014). The researcher used factors from the business environment, such as corporate branding, honors and awards, CSR policy implementation, employee training, and legal compliance, as well as factors from community development, such as youth development, environmental preservation, and upliftment of underprivileged communities, as well as CSR activities of Corporate social responsibility, to determine whether there was a relationship between various constructs. Because quasi-experimental designs typically entail pre- and post-examining the data set, correlational research design emerged as the most suited design to evaluate the relationship between constructs and variables after evaluating the various research designs (Martin & Bridgmon, 2012; Edwards-Dandridge, 2019).

3.6 DATA DESIGN

Primary and secondary data were used to understand further and examine the current study's objectives. Secondary data was gathered from various sources, including government websites, research reports, government reports, reports from research organizations, journals, journal articles, books, publications, and newspapers, among others. Moreover, primary data was collected through a self-made questionnaire and schedule based on the variables of the study, i.e., "*Corporate branding, honors and awards, implementation policy of CSR, training of employees, legal compliance and factors of community development like Youth development, preservation of nature and upliftment of the underprivileged community and CSR activities of Corporate social responsibility.*" Quantifiable studies necessitated various data-gathering strategies to examine the data variables or constructs. Haneef's study in 2013 focused on quantitative research, which is examining the relationships between constructs or variables after gathering based on a small sample size population and extrapolating the results to a larger population to develop predictions.

3.7 COLLECTION OF SECONDARY DATA

Secondary data for this research was collected from governments and private reports, including statistical reports, censuses, periodicals, magazines, thesis, books, dissertations, journals, case studies and blogs, and web information.

Collection of Primary Data

Primary data of this study was collected from the respondents of the selected area (M.P &C.G.) of the research, in which the organization's community and employees were selected.

- **Universe of the Study:** For this present Study, universes were Community people (Direct beneficiaries of CSR) and Employees (employees of that org. which comes under sec.135 Companies act 2013) of the Selected area of Study.
- **Population:** The target population explains essential information about the participants that could influence the research accuracy (Lehmann & Bengart, 2016; Edwards-Dandridge, 2019). Community people (Direct beneficiaries of CSR) and Employees (employees of that org. which comes under sec.135 Companies act 2013) from two districts of Madhya Pradesh and two districts of Chhattisgarh were considered the population of the Study. The study's sample

size was 600 In, 300 Community people, and 300 employees.

3.8 SAMPLE DESIGN

The sample design was a fundamental aspect of statistics that aid in selecting tests for the analysis. Because the researcher cannot monitor and witness all the population's responders, samples are used to gain a thorough picture of the population. As a result, sample design is a vital step for a research study since it provides a framework or blueprint that aids in selecting sample size and impacts various other critical components of the research (Lavrakas, 2008). According to Lavrakas (2008), the primary goal of sample design is to collect samples from the entire community representing the research project's population. Because sample design is the topic of some coverage to the research study population, it may be equal to the actual population size or merely a subset of the population. The sample design provides the basic concept, strategy, and approach for determining the sample size for the investigation (Lavrakas, 2008). Depending on the nature of the research, it can be very basic or highly complex (Edwards-Dandridge, 2019). The sample design for this study may be broken down into five categories: sampling method, sample unit, area specification, sample size, and participant selection. The following are some of them:

3.9 SAMPLING METHODS

The sampling method used for this study was called the connivance cum purposive sampling method. The researcher organized and arranged samples to access the current study's population, which was a purposeful and convenient sampling pattern (Leedy & Ormrod, 2001). Purposive sampling advocates and discusses focusing on a specific population with diverse or similar characteristics that can support the knowledge of the research topic and meet pre-defined study conditions (Merriam, 1998). at the same time, the convenience sampling method requirement shows the simplicity with which a population sample size can be obtained. The charge of "investigating the components of the population, the demographic sharing of the sample of the population, procuring the data set from the designated basics" is communicated by the ease of obtaining the sample (Lavrakas, 2008).

Sample Unit

The sampling unit for this research includes Community people (Direct beneficiaries of CSR) and Employees (employees of that org. which comes under sec.135 Companies act 2013) from two districts of Madhya Pradesh and two districts of Chhattisgarh to measure the correlation between the variables of Community Development and Corporate Social Responsibility.

3.10 AREA SPECIFICATION

For this study, the researcher tried to collect primary analytical data to accomplish the study's objectives, and the researcher applied a rational approach to area specification for the study.

In this way researcher selected two districts of Madhya Pradesh (Singrauli & Anuppur) and two districts of Chhattisgarh (Korba& Bilaspur)for the study. The selected area of study (Districts of States) was almost the same in the sense of Industrialisation, Socioeconomic culture, the standard of living of people, population composition, health care, and educational facilities. Researchers collect 150 valid samples from each district, with 75 respondents from Community members and 75 employees of the organizations. The total number of valid respondents was 600 for this study.

3.11 SAMPLE SIZE

An appropriate and acceptable population sample size can help to legitimize a research study by influencing the statistical outcomes of the study (Bezzina & Saunders, 2014; Edwards-Dandridge, 2019). A study with a smaller sample size may impact the study's statistical results (Sijtsma, 2016; Edwards-Dandridge, 2019). In their study, Singh and Masuku (2014) found that acquiring a sufficient sample size improves the instruments' reliability and the strength of statistical measurement outcomes. As a result, the sample size may act as an influencing factor, affecting the accuracy of the research findings. In their study, Romeo and Lee (2015) stated that sufficient sample size is crucial in generalizing a study to others. It also impacts sampling errors and confidence levels among the study's variables (Dolado et al., 2014). 2014 (Pfahler & Vukovinsky) Small sample size may reduce association strength among constructs or variables, as well as deteriorate the study's results and findings, so although a large sample may improve by removing missing values, unengaged responses, outliers, and data can take on a belly shape (normal distribution).

In contrast, small sample size may reduce association strength among constructs or variables and deteriorate the study's results and findings. For this study total proposed sample size was 700, but due to error in respondents' data, only 600 was found valid and suitable for further analysis. Of which 300 were community members and 300 were employees of different organizations. The total no of questionnaires distributed and interviews scheduled was 500 for Community members and 500 for employees of different organizations. After receiving responses and scrutinizing them, only 600 were found appropriate for the study. Missing values, unengaged responses, and outliers in the data set for the current study for 'Community development due to CSR activities 'result in data reduction.

3.12 SELECTION OF PARTICIPENTS

Selecting acceptable and eligible participants or applications can have significant (positive or negative) effects on study findings. For this study, Community people (Direct beneficiaries of CSR) and Employees (employees of that org. which comes under sec.135 Companies act 2013) of the Selected area were suitable participants. In the context of Community, member researchers try to apply a rational approach in selecting participants; in this way, the researcher selects participants from each age group based on appropriate education level; in this study, no discrimination based on caste, creed, religion, and gender. An appropriate and rational group of respondents may provide fundamental insights into Community

Development, Issues of societies, and possible solutions for the issues. On the other hand, the selection of employees was made through a rational approach, in which researchers tried to include each level of employee and each level of experience; here also, no discrimination was made based on caste, creed, religion, and gender. It was found that there were fewer participants in the female study in both community member and employee contexts. There may be many reasons behind this, and these causes are discussed further in this study.

Scale

In quantitative research, scale refers to the tools and equipment used to examine variables or constructs. After examining the information acquired with the use of scales from the respondents, quantitative research entails the predominant association among the specified variables or constructs. To achieve the study's goals, the researcher used three different scales. It has been divided into four categories: instruments used, scale adoption details, variables, and scale validity and reliability:

1.13 INSTRUMENTS UTILIZED FOR THE STUDY

Quantitative research employs a variety of scales to collect preliminary information to scrutinize proposed variables and explore existing associations between variables. The researcher can generalize findings from a subset of the target population to make predictions based on the findings. In this study, the researcher used variables of Community development like youth development, upliftment of Underprivileged communities, preservation of nature, and variables of business environment related to CSR like Corporate branding, training of employees, legal compliance, implementation policy for CSR and include the Challenge of CSR activities like political and legal challenges, financial and social challenges. These scales were utilized as the instrument for the current study to observe and measure the degree of relationship between independent and dependent variables. An independent variable predicts the relationship between a predictor variable and a predicted variable, whereas a dependent variable is the result of the predictor variables (Ko & Jeng, 2016; Edwards-Dandridge, 2019). In this study, two types of instruments were used: youth development, upliftment of Underprivileged communities, and preservation of nature; used as a parameter of Community development also measures the impact of CSR in Community Development. Business environment variable And Challenge measure positive and negative impact on CSR activities performance. In their collaborative study, Jebarajakirthy et al. (2014) argued for using categorized and authenticated research instruments in questionnaire-based research for data gathering. Similarly, (Ghosh et al., 2015; Roof, 2015) agreed that quantitative researchers could employ numerous research instruments in their investigations, and it is currently rather typical to use multiple research instruments in a quantitative study.

Variables of Instrument

Scale variables of this study were Youth Development, Upliftment of Underprivileged communities, Preservation of Nature, Corporate Branding, Training of Employees, Legal Compliance, Implementation of Policy, Political and Legal Challenges, and Financial and Social Challenges. Instruments include demographic variables like Name, Age, Gender, Education, Year of Experience.

Validity and Reliability

According to Bryman & Cramer (2003), it must be ensured that the measurement equipment is reliable and valid before a notion can be put into action. The consistency of the measure and measurement device determines the reliability. Internal and external reliability are the two types of reliability. The degree of consistency of a metric is referred to as external dependability. Internal consistency is a test or survey's internal reliability measure. Internal reliability is essential when measuring many items on a scale since it determines whether the scale is estimating a single idea or not. Consistency across items in a test is a measure of results.

According to Bryman & Cramer (2003), Cronbach's alpha helps verify the internal consistency of scales if the result is 0.8 or higher; however, Allen & Meyer (1996) indicated 0.7 as an acceptable value. The Cronbach alpha calculates reliability estimates by demonstrating that the notion and its related measure have the exact fundamental dimensions. Validity is a measure of the research's soundness. It reflects how well the notion or construct measures what it was designed to measure. Convergent and discriminant validity are construct validity subcategories. Convergent validity examines if a new scale is related to another measure in the usual way, whereas discriminative validity examines whether the notions are conceptually similar or different (Bryman & Cramer, 2003). The suitability of an instrument's measurement is determined by its validity of scale (Schaap & Kekana, 2016; Rahman et al., 2015). According to Boscart et al. (2016), valid and trustworthy equipment is critical for achieving accurate scale measurement. Similarly, emphasize the need to use a valid and reliable instrument and that using an unreliable or invalid instrument might lead to erroneous results.

Instrument Design

For a researcher Without a well-crafted questionnaire or instrument, a researcher will not be successful. However, it was regrettable that no suitable format or theoretical framework is accessible to process and design an ideal questionnaire or instrument for their research. Learning the do's and don'ts on one's own is a complex and time-consuming process that can assist the researcher in guiding the instrument's creation. As a result, creating an instrument is more of an art than a science. Designing a questionnaire is a multistage process that requires great care and attention when it comes to instrument construction. The structure of a questioner or instrument was quite tricky because it necessitates asking questions about the topics covered in the study, which differ in detail by their degree of responses. After all, questions enquired in different ways and understanding the statements led to differences in participant responses. As a result, they should pay close attention to their reactions or thoughts and how the data should be measured for analysis purposes.

Construction of Instruments

This study used two questionnaires: one for Community Members and the other for Employees. Both surveys are split into three sections, and each is described as follows: 'Introductory paragraph, Part A & Part B.'

Introduction paragraph: This questionnaire section explains the study's objective and assures respondents that their personal information will not be shared. It was an attempt to gain respondents' consent to complete the questionnaire properly and objectively.

Part A: The Demographic Profile of the Respondents is included in this section of the questionnaire.

Section B: This questionnaire section covers statements about youth development, underprivileged community uplift, environmental preservation, corporate branding, employee training, legal compliance, and implementation policy. Political and legal issues and financial and social issues are all expressed on an ordinal scale. The statements, which were placed on a five-point Likert scale and clearly explained the study's themes and closed-ended questions, were adopted and constructed to gather first-hand information. The study's goal was outlined in the s consent form and in the supporting latter, in the form of a mandated paragraph at the start of the instrument in which respondents were asked to participate and were assured of their confidentiality and privacy.

Distribution of Research Tool

Respondents or Participants were asked to complete and submit their surveys. In addition, the researcher has offered contact information to the respondents in case they have any questions, confusion, or need a substitute for collecting questionnaire forms. Most of the questionnaires were delivered to the researcher by the respondents. The data was fed into the researcher's computer; no respondents can be identified by their personal information because the researcher did not include an option to reveal their identity in the questionnaire. Every respondent has been informed and given information on the significance and relevance of the research. The researcher reassured their participants and emphasized the need for secrecy, stating that the data set's conclusions and inferences would only be used for academic research purposes.

The current study included both primary and secondary data collection approaches. For this study total proposed sample size was 700, but due to error in respondents' data, only 600 was found valid and suitable for further analysis. Of which 300 were community members and 300 were employees of different organizations. The total no of questionnaires distributed and interviews scheduled was 500 for Community members and 500 for employees of different organizations. After receiving responses and scrutinizing them, only 600 were found appropriate for the study.

Data Collection Procedure

Data collecting is usually the last step in a research project; it can be efficiently acquired by considering participant observations and interviews (Merriam & Tisdell, 2016). For this study, the researcher employed a quantitative research methodology, collected data via a paper-based and online survey, and interview schedule survey questionnaires to individuals who met the requirements within the target group. Target respondents of the study were Community members and employees of the organization of two districts of Madhya Pradesh (Singrauli & Anuppur) and two districts of Chhattisgarh (Korba& Bilaspur)for the study. The researcher also described the survey's confidentiality and anonymity. In addition, the researcher discussed the importance and demand of completed survey forms and how the researcher would eliminate and remove the incomplete survey forms. The researcher reminded the potential volunteers that participation was optional and that anyone had the right to withdraw their participation without explanation.

3.14 PILOT SURVEY

A pilot survey has been conducted to ensure that field surveys use time, effort, and money as efficiently as possible. The pilot survey allowed more thought to be given to the organization, the size of the community, and the number of employees. Before gathering data from participants or responses, a pilot test was conducted in the neighboring area. The findings of the pilot survey can be used to analyze data collection features such as data structure and time spent filling out the questionnaire. For the pilot survey, 50 structured questionnaires were received from respondents, with 25 from members of the community and 25 from employees, and were used to test the instrument's reliability. Based on Cronbach's Alpha (α) 0.757 and 0.790, it was determined that the instruments for Community members and employees were valid and consistent.

3.15 CODING OF DATA

Data coding is organizing and deducing information from collected observations or data by classifying and giving conceptual labels to empirical data based on themes and cohesive groupings. It is a procedure for "unlocking the data" (Bazeley, 2013). The researcher assigned a numeric code to the various alternatives to Community members' questions and used a survey questionnaire for further study.

Demographic Variable

Analyzing respondents' demographic profiles may provide insight into 'Community members and employees of the organization' and orientation towards Community Development. The demographic survey includes gender, age, level of education, level of designation, and experience for employees and Gender, age, and education for Community members included in the present study to determine the work and personal characteristics of the respondents. Item was analyzed based on a single question in the questionnaire, which was constructed for Community members and employees of the organization.

In the Instrument of Community member, gender, age, and educational profile were included in which male was coded with 1 and female with 2. The age of Community members was coded as 20-30 as 1, 30-40 as 2,40-50 as 3,50-60 as 4, and 60+ coded as 5. In the same way, educational profile coded as matric as1, intermediate as 2, graduate 3, P.G as4, and P. G+ coded as 5.

Tool of employees of organization Gender, Age and designation of employees, and year of experience were included in which male was coded with 1 and female with 2. Age of organization members was coded as 20-30 as 1, 30-40 as 2,40-50 as 3,50-60 as 4, and 60+ coded as 5. In the same way, Designation was coded as Foreman as1, lower-level management as 2, middle management as 3, upper management as 4, and year of experience was coded as 0-8 as1,8-16 as2, 16-24 as3,24-32 as4, and 32-40 as 5.

Likert's Scale

Questionnaire on community development, such as youth development, underprivileged community uplift, and environmental preservation. Corporate identity, Employee training and development, legal compliance, CSR policy execution, and acknowledgment of firms' performance in CSR activities. On a five-point Likert scale, this was determined. Respondents were asked to identify their feelings on the individual items or questions asked in the questionnaire on a Likert scale of Strongly Disagree = 1, Disagree = 2, Uncertain = 3, Agree = 4, and Strongly Agree = 5 to measure the above-listed factors. In the current study, two questionnaires were employed, as the researcher previously said. The Community survey instrument contains a total of 22 items or questions that are divided into numerous sub-scales and used to determine specific professional and personal characteristics of respondents. The Employees survey instrument has a total of 37 items or questions, which are divided into three self-administered multiple scales.

3.16 TECHNIQUES OF DATA ANALYSIS

The raw data was manually input and tallied from the questionnaires and schedule. The closed-ended was loaded into IBM SPSS 26 demo version to evaluate the acquired data and undertake statistical analysis. Statistical tests such as descriptive, correlation, and regression analysis are used in the study. IBM SPSS is a user-friendly statistical package that may be used to analyze descriptive and inferential statistics and determine whether null hypotheses should be accepted or rejected based on the test's significant result. The study investigated data in three phases: data cleansing in the first phase, missing data management in the second phase, and data analysis method in the third phase.

Data Cleaning

when data collection was finished, the research marked out each response set filled by respondents, excluding incomplete response sets from further analysis, intending to identify missing items. Because most software applications are built to compile the whole data set, Schafer & Graham (2002) advised that incomplete data sets be inspected, and only complete data sets are statistically analyzed. According to Osborne (2013), data cleansing is essential for improving the quality of study findings and avoiding severe inaccuracies in the results. According to Desimone et al. (2015), data screening strategies should be considered before, during, and after the survey to increase the accuracy of the research findings. He also proposed that the respondent's time spent filling out the questionnaire survey be considered and that the researcher verifies the response set for completeness. According to Hawkins (1980), outliers are data points that differ significantly from other response scores in either a positive or negative way. Measurement, sample, respondent answer, and data entry errors are the most common causes.

Missing Data

Missing data was a common concern in most studies and greatly impacted the research findings and conclusions drawn from the data. (Dorazio, 2016; Faria et al., 2014) Missing data were addressed as lacking a single or several data values for a study variable in a dataset. According to Schafer (1999), missing data in a data set has no significant impact if it is less than 5%. Bennett (2001) claimed that if a data set has more than 10% missing data, statistical analysis will produce skewed and inconsistent results. Lynch (2007) suggests assigning the median for ordinal data and mean for continuous data in missing data.

3.17 STRATEGY OF DATA ANALYSIS

Data analysis is a method for analyzing data, confirming outcomes, and producing knowledge to address a problem, not an end. Data analysis entails the critical study of data, interpretation of statistical results, and testing through figures and numbers to establish the rationale for creating significant conclusions.

The strategy of Data Analysis	
Demographic Profile of Respondents	Demographic- To explore and analyze respondents' opinions as independent variables.
Reliability Coefficient	When a construct is measured, it is crucial to determine its consistency.
Correlation	To determine the pattern of relationships between the components as well as the strength of the correlation.
Regression	To find out how independent (Predictor) factors affect dependent (Predicted) variables.

Descriptive Data Analysis

Descriptive analysis is the first step in statistical studies to describe the data's basic features. It aids in detecting outliers and identifying correlations between variables and the data distribution in this research. A comprehensive statistic about the variables and the observed data is provided by descriptive analysis. It serves as a foundation for inferential analysis.

A descriptive statistic's central tendency, spread, and dispersion are all measurements of central tendency, spread, and dispersion.

- *Central tendency*: includes the statistic such as mean, median, and mode.
- *Measures of spread*: comprise standard deviation & variance.
- *Dispersion*: defined as the range of the dataset.
- *The shape of the distribution*: introduced through skewness and kurtosis of data set.

Inferential Data Analysis

It was a statistical process for determining relationships between variables and concluding the population from a sample.

Multiple Linear Regression:

SPSS offers a variety of statistical tools and approaches to support researchers in their data analysis. Regression analysis assesses the relationships between variables or constructs and the degree to which they are related. The researcher used multiple linear regression to analyze the data set further and deduce the data set's outcomes in the current study. Multiple linear regression is a reliable and consistent statistical procedure commonly used to examine more than one independent variable and the study's dependent outcome variable (Aliahmadi et al., 2016). As a statistical tool, multiple linear regression is well suited to large sample sizes (populations) and the exploration of correlations between variables or constructs; the regression model proved to be a good and beneficial analytical method for the current study. As a result, the researcher used multiple linear regression (regression analysis) to determine if factors in the current study are significantly predicting other variables or not. The regression analysis has a distinct a dvantage over statistical data analysis techniques because it can help predict the conclusion for the predictor variables (Kam & Hamid, 2015). R, R2, and Adjusted

R2 are essential terms in multiple linear regression because they indicate the correlation coefficient, coefficient determination, and adjusted R2 (Green & Salkind, 2016; Jaseviciene & Jurksaityte, 2014). R2 denotes the strength of the variance between predictor (independent) with predicted (dependent) variables or constructs.

In contrast, adjusted R2 denotes an enhanced or revised form of R2 value that has been recalculated and adjusted for relevant predictors in the study model (Martin & Bridgmon, 2012). The adjusted R2 value, which has climbed and dropped, indicates whether the model has improved or deteriorated. Small adjusted R2 values reflect weak relationships among variables with an incapacity to anticipate the effects, whereas higher adjusted R2 values denote a significantly strong correlation with prediction competence (Wang et al., 2014). As a result, adjusted R2 advocates for a good match between the predictor and predicted variables in the model, which will help to generalize the results to the entire universe (Bakhtiari et al., 2015).

3.18 CONSTRAINS OF THE RESEARCH

Any study project has its own set of restrictions. In the case of the current study, this reduces the generalizability of the research findings, but it also makes the research more controlled and meaningful for future use. There are a few limits to this study project. The following are the details:

- For the study, two districts from Madhya Pradesh and two districts from Chhattisgarh were chosen. Most of the community was tribal and lived in small, impoverished settlements in the forest and hilly areas. As a result, due to geographical, socio-cultural, and other factors, it cannot be generalized to other MP & CG districts or the entire country.
- The sample participants of the study were chosen through a non-probability method called purposive-cum-convenient sampling.

- In this study, limited variables of Community development and Corporate Social Responsibility was considered for research; other variables like Government policies regarding Community may consider in future research.

Ethical Consideration of the Study

Sobottka (2016) highlighted the need for informed consent in social sciences and expressed serious concerns about ethical compliance. According to Humphreys (2015), Informed consent is an informal and spontaneous validation of a participant's willingness to participate in research. The researcher has obtained the required permission from responsible authorities in this study. Before enrolling potential participants, such as community members and organization personnel, the researcher has obtained their consent. Respondents' privacy was respected by the researcher, who maintained their identities and confidentiality.

3.19 CHAPTER SUMMERY

This chapter discusses the research methods, data, and statistical design employed in the study. The technique for collecting and acquiring data to satisfy the research's objectives and evaluate the hypothesized link was addressed in this chapter. The chapter discusses linear regression approaches for inferential analysis to improve the study's modeling. Through the research approach presented in this chapter, the next chapter leads to data analysis.

CHAPTER- 4

Data Analysis & Interpretation

4.1 INTRODUCTION

For This study, two significant factors have been selected: Community development and Corporate Socially Responsible. In this study, the researcher tries to find the relation and Impact of Corporate Social Responsibility initiatives on Community Development. So, the Instrument for collection of primary data has been bifurcated into two significant parts first part is related to community development which is answered by Common people of the society of the selected Area, in which questions are related to a different dimension of the community development like Youth development, poverty elevation, health care, preservation of nature, etc. The second part of the instrument is related to the organization's employees in which questions are related to different aspects of CSR, such as the impact of CSR on image building, the impact on employees, and the impact of government policies on the performance of CSR activities, etc. Collected information analysis was done through inferential Statistics like Correlation and Regression analysis. Furthermore, the null hypothesis was also tested with regression analysis.

The outcome of this primary data was interpreted, evaluated, and concluded to provide support and suggestion with a model to policymakers responsible for Community development. Also, it may be considered a helping hand for policymakers of organizations related to Corporate Social Responsibility.

4.2 PROCEDURE OF DATA REFINING

Scanning primary data was done because it's necessary to find out the out liars, missing data, incomplete data, etc. Scanning data is essential and may lead to incorrect results, hindering the study's purpose.

The preliminary information was collected from respondents (Employees and People) with the help of two separate structured questionnaires from ordinary people of the Society and Employees of the business organization to serve the purpose of the study. Later, Information was entered into SPSS 22 database and assigned the appropriate variable, label, and values.

Then After the data set has been transferred to excel for frequency test, blank and unengaged responses will be removed.

4.3 DESCRIPTIVE STATISTICS: DEMOGRAPHIC PROFILE OF RESPONDENTS

The table represents the socio-demographic representation of the respondents like Age, Gender, Educational qualification, designation of employees, etc. Responses of 300 ordinary people are recorded to serve the purpose of the study.

Table 4.1: Socio-Demographic Profile of Community people (Gender)

	Frequency	Percent	Valid Percent	Cumulative Percent
Valid Male	189	59.2	63.0	63.0
Female	111	34.8	37.0	100.0
Total	300	94.0	100.0	

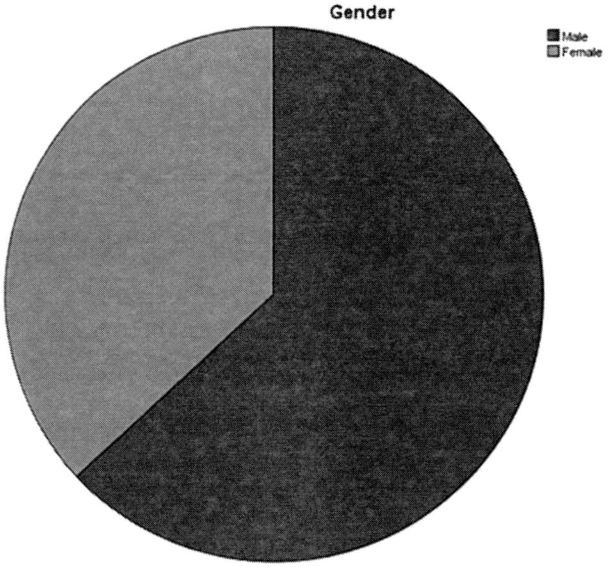

Gender bifurcated community people (Common people) in their experiences, problems, and understanding of the issues. In this data set, a total of 300 responses were found valid, and it's considered for further research; in this data set male 189(63%) and 111(37%) were recorded.

The age of respondents (Community people) is important and a key factor in understanding their issues and problems related to their community and surroundings. If the respondents are youth, they do not properly understand policy and problems. If the Respondent group are senior citizens, they also do not understand this era's current problem issues and requirements. So, in this way, it required a perfect data set with all age group respondents. Here researcher tries to cover all age group respondents. In this data set total no of respondents is 300(100%) in which 20-30 age group 42 (13.2%) 30-40age group 103(32.3%) 40-50 age group 91(28.5%)50-60 age group 47(14.7%) and 60+ 17(5.3%) was recorded. Data sets reflect that nearly 50% of respondents are under 40 and 50%are more than 40. In this way, the researcher tries to entertain the views of every age group.

Table 4.2: Socio-Demographic Profile of Community people (Age)

	Frequency	Percent	Valid Percent	Cumulative Percent
Are 20-30	42	13.2	14.0	14.0
Valid 30-40	103	32.3	34.3	48.3
40-50	91	28.5	30.3	78.7
50-60	47	14.7	15.7	94.3
60+	17	5.3	5.7	100.0
Total	300	94.0	100.0	

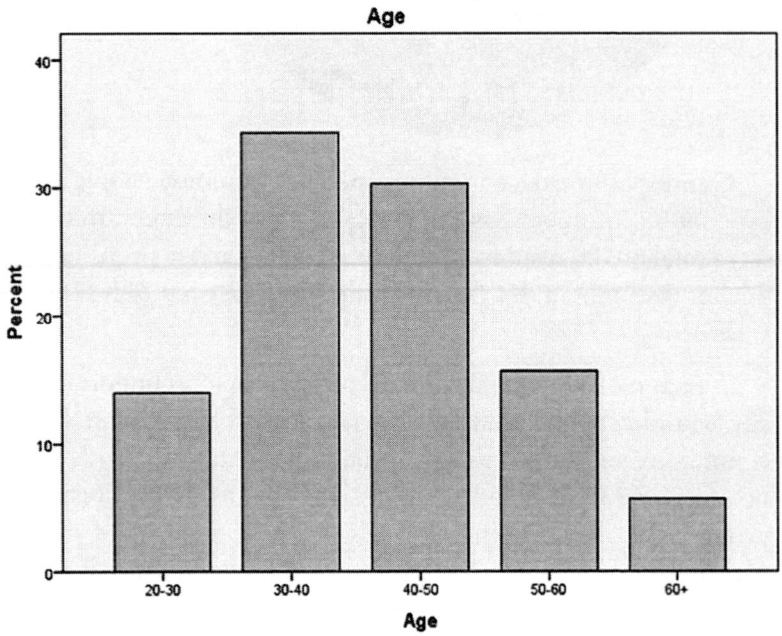

In a general scenario, educational qualification is treated as a parameter of understanding and knowledge. Educated people can understand society's real problems and responsible authorities' policies. Educated people can address society's problems, so education is one of the critical socio-demographic parameters in this data set. In this sample, graduates were 135(42.3%), intermediate

77(24.1%), Post graduates76 (23.8%), and higher studies 8(2.5%), only 4(1.3%) of respondents are matric passed out. In this data set, nearly 70% of respondents are graduate and postgraduate, so they can address the real issues of the society, understand the queries of the researcher, and respond adequately and efficiently.

Table 4.3: Socio-Demographic Profile of Community people (Education)

		Frequency	Percent	Valid Percent	Cumulative Percent
Valid	Matric	4	1.3	1.3	1.3
	Intermediate	77	24.1	25.7	27.0
	Graduation	135	42.3	45.0	72.0
	Post Graduation	76	23.8	25.3	97.3
	P.G+	8	2.5	2.7	100.0
	Total	300	94.0	100.0	

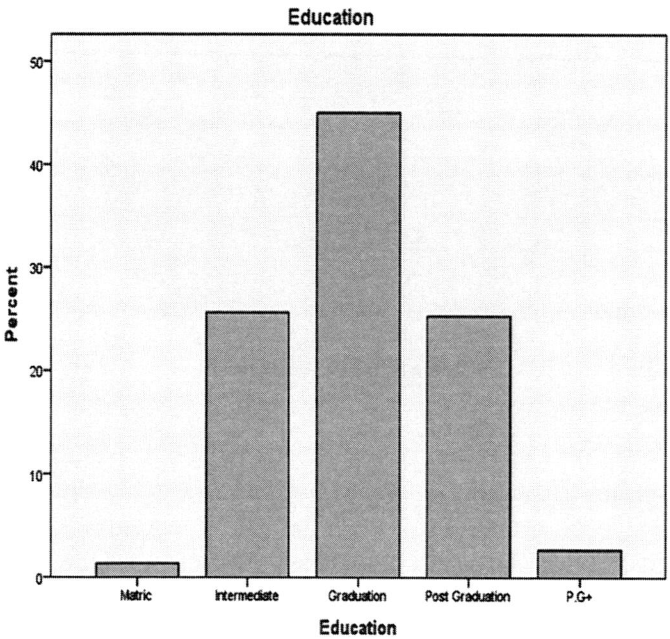

4.4 SOCIO- DEMOGRAPHIC PROFILE OF EMPLOYEES:

Further below tables and chart are represent the summery of Socio-Demographic profile of the employees of organization's related to their age, education, year of experience, designation of their work profile etc. In this data set 300 employee's responses are found valid for the further analysis.

Gender of Employee (Table 4.4)

	Frequency	Percent	Valid Percent	Cumulative Percent
Valid Male	178	58.9	59.3	59.3
Female	122	40.4	40.7	100.0
Total	300	99.3	100.0	

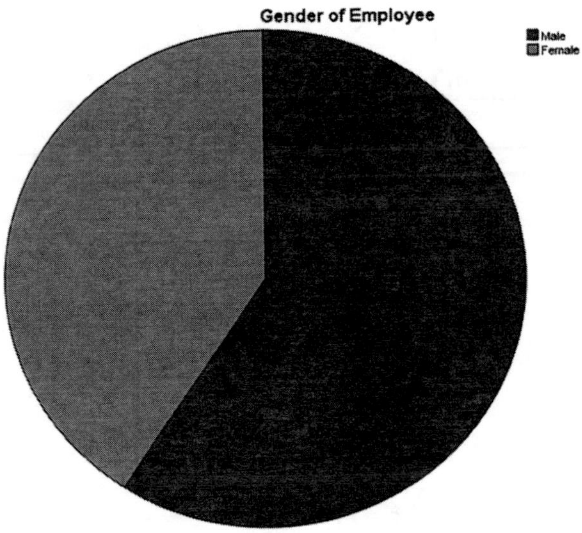

Gender bifurcation of employees shows the gender employability status of the organization; male and female orientations towards life may differ because there are many issues in society and at the workplace due to gender. So researchers try to cover the justified proportion of males and females in this way out of 300, males were 178(59.3%), and females were 122(40.7%). That shows male proportion was high in employment share.

The age of the employees is crucial because it is directly associated with their experience, which leads to the employees' attitude towards society and the organization. Researchers try to cover all possible age groups of employees to understand the organization's policies toward Corporate Social Responsibility. In this data set out of 300 respondents in which 20-30 age group 12(3%) 30-40age group 124(41.3%) 40-50 age group 121(40.3%) and 50-60 age group 46(15.3%) was recorded.

Table 4.5: Age of Employee

		Frequency	Percent	Valid Percent	Cumulative Percent
Valid	20-30	9	3.0	3.0	3.0
	30-40	124	41.1	41.3	44.3
	40-50	121	40.1	40.3	84.7
	50-60	46	15.2	15.3	100.0
	Total	300	99.3	100.0	

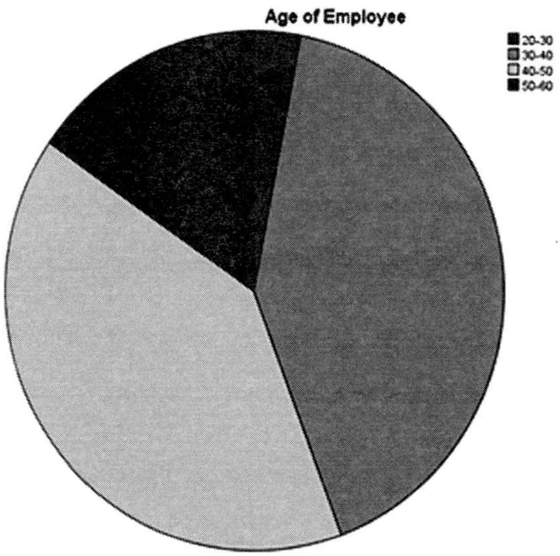

Designation of Employees also played a crucial role in understanding companies' policies and functions regarding Corporate Social Responsibility. Employees' experience on a different level of the organization was their understanding of the functions and challenges of CSR. In this way, the researcher tries to cover each level of employees; some are supervisors, some are from the middle and lower level of management, and a few are from the upper level of management. In this data set, the foreman was 119, which is 39.7% of the total sample size, lower-level management was 121which is 40.3% of the total sample size, the middle level of management was 32which is 10.7% of the total sample size, and the upper level of management was 28 which is 9.3% of total sample size was recorded.

Table 4.6: Designation of Employee

	Frequency	Percent	Valid Percent	Cumulative Percent
Valid Foreman	119	39.4	39.7	39.7
Lower management	121	40.1	40.3	80.0
Middle management	32	10.6	10.7	90.7
Upper management	28	9.3	9.3	100.0
Total	300	99.3	100.0	

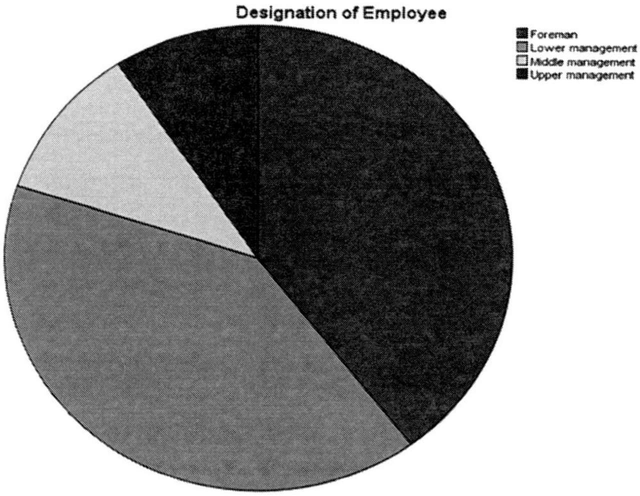

Year of Experience was a significant factor in the socio-demographic profile of employees because experience matters in analyzing the circumstances of Corporate Social Responsibility (CSR), mainly after companies act 2013 and before the act. What was the preference and mode of functioning before and after the act? In this way, the researcher can also understand the organization's challenges regarding CSR. The researcher tried to cover a reasonable sample size of each group in terms of the experience in this process total sample size is 300, in which 0-8 years of experience16(5.3%), 8-16 years of experience, 78(26%) 26-24 year of experience73(24.3%)24-32 year of experience77(25.7%) and 32-40 year of experience56(18.7%) was covered.

Table 4.7: Year of experience of Work

		Frequency	Percent	Valid Percent	Cumulative Percent
Valid	0-8	16	5.3	5.3	5.3
	08-16	78	25.8	26.0	31.3
	16-24	73	24.2	24.3	55.7
	24-32	77	25.5	25.7	81.3
	32-40	56	18.5	18.7	100.0
	Total	300	99.3	100.0	

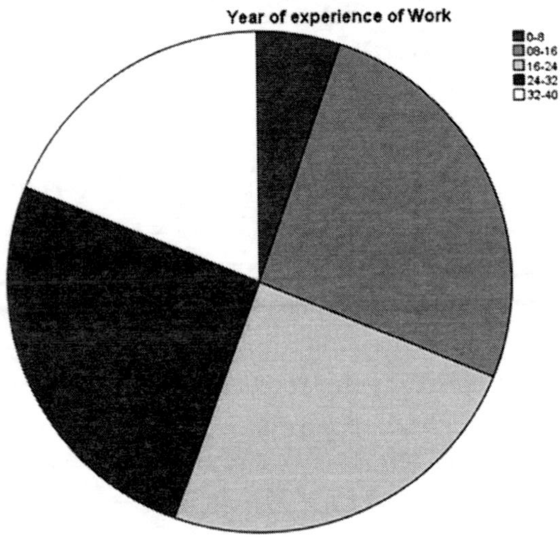

4.5 Scale Reliability &Validity Analysis (Cronbach's Alpha)

For checking internal Consistency (Reliability), Cronbach's alphA 'α' was used. Alpha value reflects that Scale was measured in the way that has meant to be measured. A high alpha value (near 1) reflected a high degree of scale consistency, meaning that the scale will be more vital. More than a .7 alpha value in social sciences is considered adequate for further statistical analysis (Cronbach, 1990).

Lower Alpha reflects that scale is unpredictable and unreliable, so valid statistical results will not produce.

In this present study, the Cronbach alpha value was used for the internal consistency and reliability of the Scale; in the present study, the scale is bifurcated into two groups. The first belongs to the Common people of Society, and the second reflects the observations of business organization employees. Both Scale was prepared and administrated by the researcher; after the data was collected from both populations, the Cronbach alpha value was calculated individually. Validity of scale was established by collecting data from 600 valid respondents, including 300 community people and 300 employees.

Table 4.8: Reliability Statistics (Community People Scale)

No of the item on the Scale	Cronbach's Alpha Value
22	.757

Table 4.9: Reliability Statistics (Employees Scale)

No of the item on the Scale	Cronbach's Alpha Value
37	.790

The scale of Community people covers some significant dimensions of community development like Youth Development, Poverty elevation, nature preservation, etc., which includes a total 22 no of questions. Their responses were collected from 300 respondents whose alpha value is (.757), which is considered significant as per the doctrine of Statistics.

In the same way scale of employees also cover some dimension of community development, Corporate Social Responsibility, and related impact on society as well as on organizations. also, in this Scale total no question was 37. The number of respondents was 300, which Cronbach's alpha value is (.790).

In Both scales, the alpha value is significant, even more than .75, which means both scales are good enough in terms of internal Consistency. Results also reflect how statements are related with purposed constructs, which also validate that respondents' responses are highly reliable.

4.6 NORMALITY TEST OF SCALE

In the process of statistical analysis, fundamental analysis tests the normality distribution of data. Normal data distribution assumes that obtained data was collected from the normally distributed population. The standard normal distribution is the most common and important distribution of probability distribution, it has a well-shaped Curve defined by its mean and standard deviation extreme value does not impact the mean value of the data set significantly.

The normality test of the dataset was crucial because it helped the researcher decide on the statistical test they use, parametric or non-parametric tests. Parametric tests like t-test, z test, f test, correlation, regression, ANOVA, etc., have basic assumptions that the data set was normally distributed. So, in this way, parametric tests require normality of data. If the data set was not normally distributed, the researcher might go for the non-parametric test.

Many tests were available for the Assessment of Assumption regarding the normality of the data set. Two primary methods are available for the assessment of normality: the graphical and the numerical method. The graphical method provides the visuals of the data set because the researcher interprets whether the data is normal or not. On the other hand, many tests and methods are available for the numerical test of normality like the Shapiro- Wilk test, Kolmogorov-Smirnov test, kurtosis, skewness, box plot, P P Plot, Q Q plot, and Z score, etc. are some methods of normality testing.

The Shapiro-Wilk test is most appropriate when n<50, although it may handle more sample sizes, the Kolmogorov-Smirnov test is appropriate for more than 50 sample sizes. Both tests have null hypotheses that the population is normally distributed when P>0.05 null hypothesis accepted data is considered as normally distributed. A dataset is considered approximately normal when kurtosis and skewness score is between -1 to +1 in case of small to moderate sample size (less than 300) less reliable because in this method Standard error is ignored, So overcome this problem Z score value is considered and z score value calculated through dividing skewness and kurtosis by their Standard Score. When (N<50) z score is (± 1.96) if the sample size is 300<N>50, then (± 3.29) is considered the normal distribution of the dataset. When N> 300, then the absolute value of skewness (±2) and kurtosis (±7) is considered for normal distribution of data. These are some assumptions about the normal distribution of data as per the doctrine of statistics (Mishra et al., 2019).

In this study, the total sample size was 600, of which 300 were community people and the rest 300 was employees of the organization, so in this way researcher considers skewness and kurtosis and z scores for the normality test of the data set.

Table 4.10: Normality test of Scale 1 (Community People)

Dimensions of tool	Skewness / Kurtosis	Standard error	Z score	Normality test
CSR activities	.305	.141	2.163	Yes
	.832	.281		
Youth Development	0.061	.141	0.432	Yes
	.205	.281		
Upliftment of Underprivileged	.228	.141	1.617	Yes
	.098	.281		
Preservation of Nature	.194	.141	1.375	Yes
	.267	.281		

Table 4.11: Normality test of Scale 2 (Employees)

Dimensions of tool	Skewness / Kurtosis	Standard error	Z score	Normality test
CSR activities	0.465	.141	-0.658	Yes
	-0.185	.281		
Honours & Awards	-0.101	.141	-0.716	Yes
	-1.081	.281		
Corporate branding	-0.239	.141	-1.76	Yes
	-0.495	.281		
Training& Awareness	-0.718	.141	0.701	Yes
	0.197	.281		
Mode of operation	0.78	.141	-2.29	Yes
	-0.645	.281		
Legal compliance	-0.127	.141	-1.82	Yes
	-0.514	.281		
Challenges	0.074	.141	-2.40	Yes
	-0.676	.281		

In testing the normality distribution of data on Scale1 (community people) and Scale 2(employees), two assumptions of normality were considered suitable for this study regarding this sample size. In this way, the researcher considered the Z Score and Absolute value of skewness and kurtosis satisfied each condition. Obtained Z score for the condition was between (± 3.29) and skewness value was under (±2), and kurtosis was also under (±7). These two Assumption of normal distribution was satisfied.

In this way Assumption of normality of the parametric test was Satisfied; further researchers may use the parametric test for hypothesis testing.

4.7 COEFFICIENTS OF CORRELATION AMONG DIFFERENT VARIABLES OF THE PROPOSED MODEL

The Coefficients of Pearson Correlation are denoted by 'r.' Pearson correlation was in signifies and measures the degree of relationship pattern and the extent of the relationship among the various variables of the study (Washington et al. 2010).

The measure of the value of Pearson correlation continuously varies between -1 to +1, which represents the degree of relationship among the variable in which a correlation value near +1 represents the positive correlation, and 0 represents no relation between variable in the same way -1 represent the negative correlation between the variables.

The degree of relationship in Coefficients of correlation is represented by its obtained value, in which a value between ±0.10 to ±0.29 represent minor effects of correlation, and a value between±0.30 to±0.50 represent the medium effects of correlation in the same way value between ±0.50 to ±1 represent the significant effects of the correlation. In This way, '+r' represents the degree of a positive relationship, which means if 1 unit increases in one variable, then the value increases in other variables in the same degree of correlation. In the same way, '-r' represent the degree of negative relation, which means if the increase in 1 degree in one variable decreases the value in the same proportion of correlation. In this study table, Pearson Correlation coefficient 'r' represents the relationship among different variables of the study. The following table expresses that there was a positive correlation among the variables.

Results and matrix of Pearson Correlation Coefficients 'r' justify the research question "To Study relationship among defined variables of the study like CSR activities, CSR challenges, Corporate branding, Youth development, Nature preservation, training, and development, etc."

The results below represent a positive correlation between CSR activities and related variables like youth development, upliftment of the underprivileged, and nature preservation; these variables depend on CSR activities. As per the results, positive and significant relations exist among the variable because r= .216**(p=.000)" Small effect Correlation" with youth development. r=.224**(p=.000)" Small effect Correlation" with the underprivileged program and r=.298**(p=.000) also have" Small effect Correlation" with nature preservation.

In the case of correlation with youth development and other variables, there was a small effect correlation with CSR Activities r= .216**(p=.000)" Small effect Correlation" with CSR activities, and medium effect correlation with both underprivileged upliftment and nature preservation where (r=.350** p=.000) (r=.307** p=.000) respectively. In the same way, privilege upliftment programs have a small effect and positive correlation with CSR activities medium effect correlation with youth development, and a significant effect correlation with nature preservation (r=.224** p=.000) (r=.350**, p=.000) (r=.587**, p=.000) respectively. In this Parlance, nature preservation Also has one small effect correlation with CSR activities (r=.298** p=.000) and has a medium effect correlation with youth development programs (r=.307** p=.000).

Table 4.12: Correlation between Purposed Model

		CSR Activities	Youth development	Under privileged upliftment	Nature preservation
CSR Activities	Pearson correlation		.216**	.224**	.298**
	Sig. (2-tailed)		.000	.000	.000
Youth development	Pearson correlation			.350**	.307**
	Sig. (2-tailed)			.000	.000
Underprivileged upliftment	Pearson correlation				.587**
	Sig. (2-tailed)				.000
Nature preservation	Pearson correlation				
	Sig. (2-tailed)				

**. Correlation is significant at the 0.01 level (2-tailed test).

In the same way, nature preservation programs significantly correlate with under-privileged upliftment where (r=.587**; p=.000).

		CSR Activities	Honors & Awards	Corporate Branding	Training & Awareness	Mode of oper ation	Legal Compl iance	Challenges
CSR Activities	Pearson correlation		.488**	.278**	.187**	.331**	.725**	.392**
	Sig. (2-tailed)		.000	.000	.000	.000	.000	.000
Honors &Awards	Pearson correlation			227**	.178**	-.007	.658**	.494**
	Sig. (2-tailed)			.000	.002	.909	.000	.000
Corporate Branding	Pearson correlation				.019	.024	.361**	.115*
	Sig. (2-tailed)				.745	.685	.000	.046
Training & Awareness	Pearson correlation					.163**	.188**	.110
	Sig. (2-tailed)					.005	.001	.056

Mode of operation	Pearson correlation						.037	.058
	Sig. (2-tailed)						.525	.317
Legal Compliance	Pearson correlation							.431**
	Sig. (2-tailed)							.000
Challenges	Pearson correlation							
	Sig. (2-tailed)							

**. Correlation is significant at the 0.01 level (2-tailed test).

*. Correlation is significant at the 0.05 level (2-tailed test).

CSR (Corporate Social Responsibility) activities depend on some factors; these factors directly or indirectly impact the policies and performance of CSR activities of organizations. In this study, the researcher tries to determine the responsible variables for CSR performance; in this way, the researcher tries to represent the relation between CSR and related variables. The above table defines that CSR activities have a positive but small effect correlation with corporate branding and training awareness programs for employees where (r=.278**; p=.000. r=187**; p=.000) respectively, and medium effect correlation with

Honors and awards, mode of operation, and Challenges of CSR where (r=.488**; p=.000. r=.331**; p=.000 r=.392**; p=.000). CSR have a positive significant effect correlation with legal compliance (r=.725**; p.000).

Same way, Honors and Awards have a Small effect correlation with corporate branding and training awareness programs for employees where (r=.227**; p=.000. r=178**; p=.002) respectively, and a medium effect correlation with CSR activities and Challenges of CSR where (r=.488**; p=.000. r=.494**; p=.000) and have positive significant effect correlation with legal compliance (r=.725**; p.000). Results show that honors and Awards have a negative correlation with the mode of operation, but that was insignificant (r=-.007; r=.909). Corporate branding positively correlates with legal compliance and challenges (r=.361**; p=.000) (r=.115**; p=.046). Training and awareness of employees have a small effect correlation with Mode of operation and legal compliance with (r=.163** p=.005and.188** p=.001) respectively. In the same parlance, legal requirements of CSR have a positive medium effect correlation with Challenges of CSR where the value of r is .431** and p is (.000).

4.8 REGRESSION ANALYSIS AMONG DIEFFENRT VARIABLES OF PROPOSED MODEL

Variables (predictor variable) over the dependent variable (predicting variables) were analyzed using statistical software SPSS. Regression value may also be considered for the model fit; based on regression results, it can predict the rationality and validity of multiple linear regression models. In the summary of regression model values included, R represents (correlation coefficients) the linear association among the dependent variable and their independent variables, and R^2 represents (Coefficients of determination) variance proportion of independent variable defining the dependent variable. Adjusted R^2 was used to recalculate the R^2 value for the influence of predictor variable has on the R^2 Value (Field,2013). With this value, the Durbin Watson test was also used to determine autocorrelation, also known as Serial correlation. If data was collected from the same source for the same objective, then there was a correlation, and if these conditions were fulfilled, no auto correlation or serial correlation was found. In this study, the Dublin Watson test value was between 1 and 3, which is enough to fulfill the regression analysis assumptions requirements. If the test value was lower than 1 or more than3, there was a consecutive correlation between the observations (Garson, 2012).

In the regression analysis process, research software (SPSS) does not allow more than one dependent variable because this researcher must bifurcate the hypothesis in sub hypothesize to accomplish the purpose of the study. In this way, a central hypothesis is bifurcated into sub hypothesis like this:

$H_0$1: There exists no significant role of corporate social responsibility activities on community development.

$H_0$1a: There is no significant role of CSR activities on youth development.

$H_0$1b: CSR activities have no significant role for underprivileged communities.

$H_0$1c: There is no significant role of CSR activities in Nature preservation.

$H_0$2: Business Environment Variables do not have a significant impact on the CSR activities of the organization.

$H_0$2a: Honor and awards do not impact CSR activities performance

$H_0$2b: corporate branding does not have a significant impact on the CSR activities of the organization.

$H_0$2c: Training and awareness program of employees does not impact CSR activities performance.

$H_0$2d: Mode of operation does not impact CSR activities performance

$H_0$2e: legal compliance does not impact CSR activities' performance

$H_0$3: Challenges do not impact the delivery of CSR activities in community development.

$H_0$3b: Government policies do not significantly impact CSR activities.

$H_0$3c: Community pressure does not significantly impact CSR activities.

$H_0$3d: Financial challenges do not have a significant impact on CSR activities.

$H_0$3e: Political pressure does not significantly impact CSR activities.

Table 4.13: Regression Analysis Between Purposed Model

Proposed model summery

			R	R square	Adjusted R square	t	Sig.	Durbin Watson
No.	**Independent variable**	**Dependent variables**						
1.	Predictors (Constant) : CSR	Youth Development	.216a	.047	.044	3.823	.000	2.056
		Under Privileged	.224a	.050	.047	3.963	.000	2.016
		Nature Preservation	.298a	.089	.086	5.391	.000	2.186
2	Honor& Awards	CSR Activities	.488a	.238	.236	9.652	.000	1.481
	Corporate branding		.278a	.078	.074	5.005	.000	1.133
	Training& Awareness		.187a	.035	.032	3.287	.001	1.000
	Mode of operation		.331a	.110	.107	6.059	.000	.855
	Legal compliance		.725a	.525	.523	18.151	.000	1.717
3	Challenges	CSR Activities	.442a	.196	.193	8.510	.000	1.404
	Challenges of GOVT. policies		.168a	.028	.025	2.936	.004	.919
	Challenges of Community pressure	CSR activities	.201a	.040	.037	3.537	.000	1.062
	Challenges of a financial crisis		.071a	.005	.002	1.236	.217	.963
	Challenges of political pressure		.181a	.033	.030	3.185	.002	.922

The above table represents the summary of regression analysis for the proposed model, and many linear regression equations were tested to test the hypothesis mentioned above and sub hypothesis. As mentioned above, three model summaries were tabulated because three models and analyses were done in three phases. First model summary $\mathbf{H_01}$ represent the Significant impact of CSR activities over the variables of Community development with their adjusted R^2 Values on Youth development **($\mathbf{H_01a}$**;0.044*) provision for the Underprivileged (**$\mathbf{H_01b}$**;0.047) and significantly impact the provision for nature preservation (H_01c;0.086). Second model summary H02 represents the Significant impact of different variables on the CSR activities of the organization like honors &Awards, significantly impacting CSR activities where Adjusted R^2 Value (H_02**a**; 0.236). Corporate branding of the organization may also impact CSR activities, and it was proved with their adjusted R^2 Values (**$\mathbf{H_02b}$**;0.074) and training and awareness of the employees towards the CSR activities also significantly impact on CSR activities it was shown as (**$\mathbf{H_02c}$**;0.032) in same way mode of operation of CSR activities is also impact on the performance of CSR activities it was shown (**$\mathbf{H_02d}$;**0.107) legal compliance or guidelines of Government also impact on performance on organizations CSR activities its shown in (**$\mathbf{H_02e}$;**0.523). Third model Summery H_03 impact of those challenges was measured with their adjusted R^2 Values (**$\mathbf{H_03a}$;** 0.193) in the same way challenges of Government policies significantly impact CSR activities (**$\mathbf{H_03b}$;** 0.025). Community pressure also has an impact on CSR activities, as shown in (**$\mathbf{H_03c}$;** 0.037). The financial crisis was not significantly impacting the CSR activities shown in (**$\mathbf{H_03d}$;** 0.002), but the same challenges of political pressure significantly impacted CSR activities performance represented in (**$\mathbf{H_03e}$;** 0.030).

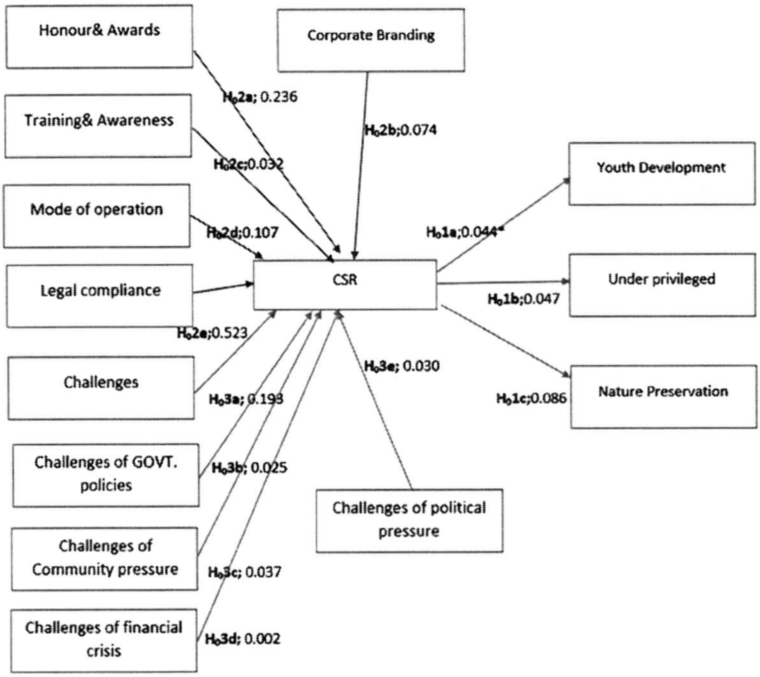

In this purposed model, parameters were weighted with the hypothesis and with the adjusted R^2 Significance value, which was calculated through linear regression path analysis, leading to a refined measurement model represented through multiple regression analysis with inclusion of overall variables of the model, where adjusted R^2 reflects the contribution or impact of independent or exogenous variables on predicting variables for this study.

In this research, Corporate Social responsibility significantly impacts the selected variables of Community development like youth development, upliftment of the underprivileged community, and preservation of nature and heritage. On the other hand, CSR was impacted by various variables like corporate branding, training and development of employees, mode of operation for CSR activities, legal Compliance, and honors &awards. In the same way, some challenges like political and community pressure and government policies significantly impact CSR activities, but financial crisis challenges do not significantly impact CSR activities.

4.9 HYPOTHESIS TESTING

The researcher has framed many hypotheses after analyzing the research question and objectives of the study. In this way researcher framed three hypotheses to serve the purpose of the study. All those hypotheses were tested through Regression analyses and after applying a t-test. Results of the hypotheses were elaborated below:

The first hypothesis, **$H_0$1, "There exists no significant role of corporate social responsibility activities on community development."** This hypothesis was further classified into sub-hypotheses with the selected variable of Community development as H01a, H01b, and H01c to test the individual effect of CSR activities on variables of Community development, respectively, Youth development, upliftment of privileged, and nature preservation. Results of the test represented through the following table that confirms or validates the predictor variable CSR significantly predicted youth development $H_0$1a (**Adj. R^2=0.044 t=3.823 sig=.000) Underprivileged $H_0$1b** (**Adj. R^2=0.047 t=3.963 sig=.000)** and Nature preservation $H_0$1c (**Adj. R^2=0.086 t=5.391 sig=.000**) based on results of sub hypotheses $H_0$1 "*There exist no significant role of corporate social responsibility activities on community development.*" was **rejected.**

Second hypothesis **$H_0$2: "Business Environment Variables does not significantly impact on CSR activities of the organization."** To validate the hypothesis was further classified into sub-hypotheses with selected variables as H02a, H02b, H02c, H02d, and H02e. To test of individual effects of variables of business environment on CSR activities. Results of the test presented through the table that confirms or validate the predictor variable honor& Awards significantly predict the CSR performance $H_0$2a (Adj. R^2=0.236 t=9.652 sig=.000) The predictor variable corporate branding predicts the CSR performance H02b (**Adj. R^2=0.074 t=5.005**

sig=.000) the predictor variable training & awareness predict the CSR performance $H_0$2c (**Adj. R^2=0.032 t=3.287 sig=.001**) the predictor variable mode of operation predict the CSR performance $H_0$2d (**Adj. R^2=0.107 t=6.059 sig=.000**) and the predictor variable legal compliance predict the CSR performance $H_0$2e (**Adj. R^2=0.523 t=18.151 sig=.000**) on the basis on results of sub hypotheses H02: "*Business Environment variables do not significantly impact on CSR activities of the organization*" was **rejected**.

Many challenges directly or indirectly impact CSR performance in the performance of CSR activities. In this way, to measure the impact of those challenges, the third hypothesis was framed as **$H_0$3: "Challenges do not impact the delivery of CSR activities in community development."** Furthermore, this was bifurcated into sub-hypotheses as $H_0$3a, $H_0$3b, $H_0$3c, $H_0$3d, and $H_0$3e, and These hypotheses were tested. Results were shown through the table in which predictor variable was other challenges of organizations that predict the CSR performance as $H_0$3a (**Adj. R^2=0.193 t=8.510 sig=.000**). After that, Predictor variable challenges of Govt. policies predict the CSR performance $H_0$3b (**Adj. R^2=0.025 t=29.36 sig=.004**) predictor variable challenges of community pressure predicts the CSR performance $H_0$3c (**Adj. R^2=0.037 t=3.537 sig=.000**) in this way predictor variable challenges of financial crisis does not predicts the CSR performance $H_0$3d (**Adj. R^2=0.002 t=1.236 sig=.217" not significant"**) and predictor variable challenges of political pressure predicts the CSR performance $H_0$3e(**Adj. R^2=0.030 t=3.185 sig=.002**) on the basis of above results of sub hypotheses *H03: "Challenges do not impact on the delivery of CSR activities in community development.*" was **partially rejected**.

Table 4.14: Hypothesis Testing

Hypothesis		Accepted/ Rejected	Sig.	Test techniques
H01	**There exists no significant role of corporate social responsibility activities in community development**	**Rejected**		**Regression Analysis**
H01a	there is no significant role of CSR activities on youth development	Rejected	.000	
H01b	there is no significant role of CSR activities towards underprivileged communities.	Rejected	.000	
H01c	there is no significant role of CSR activities in Nature preservation.	Rejected	.000	
H02	**Business Environment Variables do not significantly impact on CSR activities of the organization**	**Rejected**		**Regression Analysis**
H02a	Honor and awards do not impact CSR activities' performance	Rejected	.000	
H02b	corporate branding does not have a significant impact on the CSR activities of the organization	Rejected	.000	

H02c	Training and awareness program for employees does not impact CSR activities' performance	Rejected	.001	
H02d	Mode of operation does not impact CSR activities' performance	Rejected	.000	
H02e	Legal challenges do not impact CSR activities' performance	Rejected	.000	
H03	**Challenges do not impact the delivery of CSR activities in community development**	**Partially Rejected**		**Regression Analysis**
H03a	Other Challenges do not impact the delivery of CSR activities in community development	Rejected	.000	
H03b	Government policies do not have a significant impact on CSR activities	Rejected	.004	
H03c	Community pressure does not have a significant impact on CSR activities	Rejected	.000	
H03d	A financial crisis does not have a significant impact on CSR activities	Not Rejected	.217	
H03e	Political pressure does not have a significant impact on CSR activities	Rejected	.002	

4.10 CONCLUSION

This chapter started with analyzing the demographic profile of the respondents from Community members And Employees of organizations in the Selected Area of Study. After that, the reliability and validity of the tools were measured. The normality of the data set was checked based on Skewness/kurtosis and Z score value; after that, correlation Analysis and Dublin Watson test were performed to fulfill the regression analysis assumptions. After that, the regression test was performed, then the theoretical model was tested with linear regression path analysis, and regression analyses validated the research hypothesis.

CHAPTER- 5

Findings, Suggestions, Limitations, and Conclusion

5.1 INTRODUCTION

The selected topic of this research Corporate Social Responsibility and its impact on community development was a very dynamic subject. It involves multi-dimensions of human interactions and many environments related to human society like political environment, economic environment, Socio-cultural environment, and natural environment. This study was empirically analyzed with the help of a data set and different statistical test results based on the different construct of CSR dimensions like CSR impact on Society, Impact on Nature, Impact on employees, and impact on profitability. CSR performance, issues, challenges of CSR activities, and exact ways Dimensions of Community development include youth development, nature preservation, and upliftment of underprivileged society.

This chapter was broadly summarized under the four headings Finding, Suggestion, Limitation, and Conclusion. In which findings were drawn with the help of Statistical test results and hypothesis testing of this data set. After finding, the researcher tried to make some helpful policy-making suggestions based on statistical results for the policy maker and other stakeholders of the CSR activities. After that, all conclusion was drawn point-wise. In the same way, limitations of the study were drawn in which the researcher attempted to address the issues and challenges of the study like data collection visiting the study area, and others.

5.2 FINDINGS

Findings are the Fundamental outcomes of the study, which were extracted from the data set of study by interpretation of hypothesis testing and statistical test results. In this research, findings are categorized in different subheadings like demographic findings, reliability test, normality test correlation, regression test, model testing, etc. findings are as follows:

Findings related to Descriptive analysis

In this descriptive analysis section, the researcher also analyzed the demographic profile of the Community people and organizations' respondents. Findings are as follows:

Demographic findings of Community

Analysis of table and pie chart (4.1) related to the gender of the community people in which 300 responses were valid in which 67 % were male, and the rest of 37% was female. This means that in the selected Society, the male respondents gave more valid responses than females. Many factors were responsible for this difference, like the reach of respondents, understanding of questions, hesitation, social barrier, education, etc. That may be reduced in the future if responsible authorities for policy-making take corrective action and other stakeholders of society like educational institutions and policy implementing systems also become responsible and more accountable.

Analysis of (table 4.2) related to the **age** of respondents (Community people) was important and a key factor for understanding their issues and problems related to their community and surroundings. If the respondents are only youth, they do not properly understand policy and problems. If the Respondent group are senior citizens, they also do not understand this era's current problem issues and requirements. So, in this way, it required a perfect data set with all age group respondents. Here researcher tries to cover all age group respondents. In this data set total no of respondents is 300(100%) in which 20-30 age group 42 (13.2%) 30-40age group 103(32.3%) 40-50 age group 91(28.5%)50-60 age group 47(14.7%) and 60+ 17(5.3%) was recorded. Data sets reflect that nearly 50% of respondents are under 40 and 50%are more than 40.

Analysis of (Table 4.3) related to **Educational Qualification** in common scenario educational qualification is treated as the parameter of understanding and knowledge. Educated people can understand society's real problems and responsible authorities' policies. Educated people can address society's problems, so education is one of the essential socio-demographic parameters in this data set. In this research, graduate respondents were 135(42.3%), intermediate 77(24.1%) Post graduates76 (23.8%), and higher studies 8(2.5%), only 4(1.3%) of respondents are matric pass out. In this data set, about 70% of respondents are graduate and postgraduate, so they can address the real issues of the society, understand the researcher's queries, and respond adequately and efficiently.

Demographic Findings of Employees of the organization

Analysis of (table 4.4) related with Gender in which bifurcation of employees shows the gender employability status in the organizations, it's also show male and female orientation towards life may differ from each other because there are many issues in society as well as at the workplace due to gender inequality. So, the researcher tried to cover the justified proportion of males and females in this way out of 300 total respondents, the male was 178(59.3%), and female were 122(40.7%). That shows male proportion was high in employment share. There were many responsible factors for this difference like the nature of work of the selected organization, Socio-cultural factors, Training and awareness, education status, etc.

Policy improvements, awareness programs, motivation Programs, and reservations may also be helpful in this situation.

Analysis of (table and pie chart 4.5) which is related to **Age** of the employees is crucial because it is directly associated with the employees' experience, which leads to the employees' attitude towards society and organization. Researchers try to cover all possible age groups of employees to understand the organization's policies toward Corporate Social Responsibility. This data set out of 300 respondents bifurcated among five groups the 20-30 age group, 12(3%) 30-40age group, 124(41.3%), 40-50 age group, 121(40.3%), and 50-60 age group 46(15.3%) was recorded. The different age groups have different understanding and senses towards the problems and solutions, and they also have different kinds of orientation toward its organization and society. This way, the researcher tries to engage different age groups to obtain an accurate outcome.

Analysis of (table and pie chart 4.6) related with **Designation of Employees, which also played a** crucial role in understanding companies' policies and functions regarding Corporate Social Responsibility. What was the experience of employees on a different level of the organization? What was their understanding regarding the functions and challenges of CSR? This way, the researcher tried to cover each level of employees; some were supervisors, some from a middle and lower level of management, and a few from the upper level. In this way, the data set was comprised like this which foreman was 119, which is 39.7% of the total sample size, lower-level management was 121which is 40.3% of the total sample size, the middle level of management was 32which is 10.7% of the total sample size and from the upper level of management was 28 which is 9.3% of total sample size was recorded. In this data set, participation of upper and middle-level management was comparatively low; there were many responsible reasons behind this, like workload of employees, sometimes policy matters, availability of time, etc.

Analysis of (table and pie chart 4.7) which is related to **Year of Experience of employees** was also a crucial factor in terms of socio-demographic profile of employees because the experience was very crucial in terms of analyzing the circumstances of Corporate Social Responsibility (CSR), mainly after companies act 2013 and before the act. What was the preference and mode of functioning before and after the act? In this way, the researcher may also understand the organization's challenges regarding CSR. The researcher tried to cover a reasonable sample size of each group in terms of the experience in this process total sample size was 300, with which 0-8 years of experience16(5.3%), 8-16 years of experience, 78(26%) 26-24 year of experience73(24.3%)24-32 year of experience77(25.7%) and 32-40 year of experience56(18.7%) was covered. In this study, more than 50% of employees have more than 25 years of experience, so they also have experience of change in society and working in an organization. In this way, experienced employees may give more realistic insights into the CSR policy and its implementation and outcomes.

5.3 FINDING RELATED TO RELIABILITY ANALYSIS

Reliability analysis was directly associated with the analysis of scale consistency which reflects the construct's validity and reliability. For checking internal Consistency (Reliability), Cronbach's alpha 'α' was used. Alpha value reflects that Scale was measured in the way that has meant to be measured.

In this study, there was two-scale for the measurement in which the Scale of Community people cover some significant dimensions of community development like Youth Development, Poverty elevation, nature preservation, etc., which includes a total 22 no. of questions, and their responses were collected from 300 respondents that alpha value is (.757) which considered significant as per the doctrine of Statistics.

In the same way scale of employees also cover some dimension of community development, Corporate Social Responsibility, and related impact on society as well as on organizations. also, in this Scale total no question was 37. Respondents were 300, which Cronbach's alpha value is (.790).

In Both scales, the alpha value is significant, even more than .75, which means both scales are good enough in terms of internal Consistency. Results also reflect how statements are related to purposed constructs. These results also validate that respondents' responses are highly reliable.

5.4 FINDING RELATED TO NORMALITY ANALYSIS

The normality test of the dataset was crucial because it helped the researcher decide on the statistical test they wanted to use, whether parametric or non-parametric. Parametric tests like t-test, z test, f test, correlation, regression, ANOVA, etc., assume that the data set was normally distributed. So in this way, parametric tests require a normality test of data; if the data set was not generally distributed, then the researcher may go for the non-parametric test.

Many tests were available for the Assessment of Assumption regarding the normality of the data set. Two primary methods are available for the assessment of normality: the graphical and the numerical method. The graphical method provides the visuals of the data set because the researcher interprets whether the data is standard or not. On the other hand, many tests and methods are available for the numerical test of normality like the Shapiro- Wilk test, Kolmogorov-Smirnov test, kurtosis, skewness, box plot, P P Plot, Q Q plot, and Z score etc. are some methods of normality testing. The normality test methods depend on sample size and the study's requirements.

In this study, the total sample size was 600, of which 300 were community people and the rest 300 were employees of the organization, so in this way researcher considers skewness and kurtosis and z scores for the normality test of the data set. In testing the normality distribution of data on Scale1 (community people) and Scale 2(employees), two assumptions of normality were considered suitable for this study regarding this sample size. In this way, the researcher considered the Z Score and Absolute value of skewness and kurtosis satisfied each condition. Obtained Z score for the condition was between (± 3.29) and skewness value was under (±2), and kurtosis was also under (±7). Assumptions of normal distribution were satisfied.

In this way, the Assumption of the parametric test's normality was Satisfied, so the researcher used the parametric test for the hypothesis testing.

5.5 FINDING RELATED TO CORRELATION ANALYSIS

Correlation analysis was essential for measuring cause and effects relationship among the study variable. The correlation value represents the degree of association, and its also important because it is a basic assumption for regression analysis. In this, it's found that there was a significant linear relationship between the CSR activities and different variables of community development like Youth development, nature preservation, and upliftment of the underprivileged community. Furthermore, there was a range of small effect correlation to medium-range correlation, and a significant effect correlation was found, which is enough for further regression analysis (Table 4.12). Further, a significant correlation was found between youth development and nature preservation. After that, a medium effect correlation was found between youth development and upliftment of underprivileged communities. Also, there seems to be a strong relationship between the upliftment of underprivileged communities and nature preservation. In this way, youth development is helpful in uplifting society and nature preservation. When underprivileged community status changes, it leads to nature preservation; according to this dataset, there was a chain of development. (Table 4.12)

After that, the results of correlation analysis consolidate the idea that Corporate Social Responsibility activities may be affected by other variables like honor &Awards, Corporate branding, training, and development mode of operation of CSR activities, and Legal Compliance. Furthermore, it found that CSR activities have a medium effect correlation with honors and awards, which means recognition of organizations positively affects CSR activities. After that, CSR has a low correlation with corporate branding and pieces of training and development of the employees, which means, according to this data set, corporate branding is not significant in CSR activities. However, legal compliance strongly correlates with CSR activities which means the provision of sec.135 of Companies act 2013 is strongly affected in terms of CSR activities. Further, legal compliance also has a strong correlation with honors and awards, which means legal compliance leads to CSR activities and recognition of the organization. (Table 4.12)

Further in the process of Correlation analysis, it found that CSR activities performance is also affected by some other negative factors like political pressure, Community pressure, financial crisis, challenges due to legal compliance, and other factors. Furthermore, it found that all these variables have a small to medium effect correlation with CSR activities except for financial crisis hindrance.

In the correlation analysis, it was substantiated that CSR activities have a crucial role in the development of society, and CSR was also affected by many variables of the internal business environment and external environment.

5.6 FINDING RELATED TO REGRESSION ANALYSIS

Regression analysis was carried out to analyze the validity of hypotheses, assumptions, and validity of the study's objective Regression analysis was done, and it validated the proposed conceptual models, which were based on three main hypotheses and 14 sub hypotheses; multiple regression analysis was done, which led to the three regression models.

In the first regression model (Table 4.13), Corporate Social Responsibility activities are considered predictor, and variables of community development like youth development, upliftment of the underprivileged community, and nature preservation was the predicted variable. Where 't' value was significant, it was inferred that CSR activities of corporate organizations predicted Youth development by 4.4% (adjusted R2 value), upliftment of underprivileged communities by 4.7 %, and nature preservation by 8.6 %. That means authorities were responsible for CSR policy-making and its implementation. That requires more efficiency and effectiveness; for this, they may change their policies of implementation, policies of priorities, train and motivate employees towards CSR activities, and research other causes. On the other hand, Governments may also change the policy of priorities by researching and fixing the accountability of the authorities and organizations responsible for it.

In second regression model (Table 4.13) researcher try to analyse external business environment factors and internal business environment factors those are responsible for affecting performance of CSR activities in this way Honours and Awards consider as predictor and CSR activities of the organization considered as predicted variable and it was found that Honour & awards predict CSR activities by 23.6% (adjusted R2 value), again Corporate Branding consider as predictor and CSR activities of the organization considered as predicted variable and results shows that CSR was predicted with Corporate branding by 7.4% Again Training of employees consider as predictor and CSR activities of the organization considered as predicted variable and it was found that training of employees predict CSR activities by 3.2 % than after Mode of Operation CSR activities consider as predictor and CSR activities of the organization considered as predicted variable and results reflect that mode of implementation of CSR activities predict CSR activities by 10.7% after that Legal Compliance consider as predictor and CSR activities of the organization considered as predicted Variable and results reflect that CSR activities was predicted by legal Compliance with 52.3% and in all above sub models of second model 't' value was found significant. Regression analysis results of the second model show the internal and external environment variables. Significantly predicts CSR activities performance, as results show that Honours &Awards and legal compliance was significantly predicted CSR activities it means recognition of organizations and sec 135 of companies' act 2013 may improve the performance of the CSR activities both belong to the external environment. Results also show a requirement to improve organizations' internal environments toward CSR activities.

In Third regression model of study researcher analyses the hindrances of external and internal business environment those are impact on CSR activities of organization in this way Challenges of Government policies was consider as predictor variable and CSR activities was consider as predicted variable results shows that CSR activities was predicted by policy challenges by 2.5% (adjusted R2 value), and again changes Community pressure was consider as predictor variable and CSR activities was consider as predicted variable results shows that CSR activities was predicted by 3.7% again challenges of financial crisis was consider as predictor variable and CSR activities was consider as predicted variable results shows that CSR activities was predicted by 0.2% after that political pressure was consider as predictor variable and CSR activities was consider as predicted variable results shows that CSR activities was predicted by 3% and after that other challenges was consider as predictor variable and CSR activities was consider as predicted variable results shows that CSR activities was predicted by 19.3 % and in all above cases 't' value was found Significant. Results of the third regression model reflect those external environmental challenges like political challenges, community pressure, or policy-related somehow impact CSR activities performance. However, the financial crisis was not impacting significantly on CSR activities, which means in terms of CSR activities, finance was not a significant problem, but external pressure impacted the performance of CSR activities. There was a need to overcome those problems for these business organizations and government should take corrective action regarding policy making and implementation.

5.7 FINDING RELATED TO HYPOTHESIS TESTING

In the process of fulfilling the objectives of the study, many research question was framed. A question hypothesis was formed after regression analysis was done to validate the hypothesis and fulfill the study's objectives.

Results of framed hypothesis testing and findings were presented in table 4.14, and outcomes and interpretation were as follows:

The hypothesis was validated based on obtained significant 't' value. In this way, there was a significant 't' value obtained for the variables of Community Development like youth development, upliftment of the underprivileged community, and nature preservation, so all sub thesis of the first hypothesis was rejected it means $H_0$1 "*There exist no significant role of corporate social responsibility activities on community development.*" was **rejected**. That means CSR activities of an organization has significant upon select variables of the Community development, i.e., Youth development, upliftment of the underprivileged community, and nature preservation (H01 rejected for Youth development, upliftment of the underprivileged community, and nature preservation, hence 'reject' expression was used in terms of validating $H_0$1) (Table4.14).

Based on obtained significant 't' value of sub hypothesis of the second hypothesis in which positive factors of the internal and external business environment, i.e., corporate branding, Honours& Awards, Training & Awareness, Mode of operation, and legal Compliance, were considered independent (predictor) and Corporate social responsibility consider as dependent variable (predictable variable). $H_0$2 "Business Environment Variables does not significantly impact on CSR activities of the organization" was rejected. That reflects that CSR activities performance was affected by business environment variables like corporate branding,

Honours& Awards, Training & Awareness, Mode of operation, and Legal Compliance. In this way, the 'Rejected' expression was used in presenting the validity of $H_0$2 (Table4.14).

The third hypothesis of the study was also validated based on obtained significant 't' value, in which Challenges related to the business environment like political pressure, financial crisis, community pressure, legal compliance, and other challenges consider as the independent variable (predictor). Corporate Social Responsibility activities of the organization were considered a dependent variable (predictable). Based on obtained 't' value $H_0$3: "*Challenges does not impact on the delivery of CSR activities in community development.*" was **partially rejected**. Test results show that political pressure, community pressure, legal compliance, and other challenges significantly impact the performance of CSR activities, but a financial crisis does not significantly impact CSR activities. In this way, $H_0$3d "*Financial crisis does not significantly impact on CSR activities*" was 'not rejected' (Table 4.14). So H03 was rejected for the political pressure, community pressure, legal compliance, and other challenges but not rejected for the Financial Crisis. Hence 'A partially rejected' expression was used to validate the third hypothesis ($H_0$3 "*Challenges do not impact on the delivery of CSR activities in community development.*")

5.8 SUGGESTIONS & RECOMMENDATIONS

Suggestions and recommendations both are indicative and expressive. Moreover, both are crucial for the policymakers of the related subject and also very essential for other stakeholders like Community people, Organizations, Governments, etc. Recommendation and Suggestive statements are derived from experience, experiments, observation, or analysis. The present study recommends suggestions based on statistical data set analysis. Moreover, their interpretations are based on the researcher's observation and experience.

5.8.1 Suggestions

The present study was conducted to analyze the role of Corporate Social Responsibility Activities in Community Development. Three main variables of Community development were selected, and the researcher also included business environment factors responsible for CSR activities' performance. So, a Suggestion was made on that basis. Some suggestions are as follows:

- Organizations should encourage employees to train & development for CSR activities and also conduct a more intensive program for training. It helps develop employees on a professional and personal level, which may lead to increased employee competency, which helps increase the effectiveness of CSR policy recommendations that lead to community development and corporate branding.
- In the Selected area of research, it was found that there was significant gender inequality in the community. In employability, for this there were many responsible factors like education of girls, socio-cultural barriers, socio-economic factors, traditions, and faith of the community, etc. to overcome this inequality, there was a need for policy evaluation and change, it has also recommended that conducting motivation program at the organization level and Government level.
- It was experienced that illiteracy and educational backwardness was significant problem in the selected area, so in policy making of CSR activities for community development, educational development must be a crucial factor because education leads to overall human development that leads to Community development.
- The selected area of this study was primarily rural, and people mainly belong to deprived sections of society; they are tribes and Schedule cast. Tribes mostly live in forests and hilly areas and have different traditions and rituals. In this way, geographical and socio-cultural factors play a crucial role in the community's backwardness, so the area of

study needs particular policy and procedure for community development.

- It was experienced that there was a Scarcity of necessities for community people like potable water, medical facilities, educational facilities, and employability; in this way, CSR policy in this area must prioritize the factors of necessities. It also recommended that government prioritize these factors, ensure the effective implementation of policy, and ensure the accountability of responsible authorities.
- Results show that CSR activities such as youth development, nature preservation, and upliftment of underprivileged communities play a significant role. However, the impact of CSR activities was not promising. So, a business organization must ensure the effectiveness of CSR activities and increase the proportion of CSR activities in Community development.
- Mode of operation has a significant impact on CSR activities, so business organizations must ensure the implementation of CSR policies time its required direct and sometimes indirect implementation.
- Organizations may also appoint a marketing team in Corporate Social Responsibility that leads accomplishment of the objective of CSR policy and increase the effectiveness of CSR activities that must lead the Corporate Branding, which is a significant factor in sale turnover and profitability of organizations.
- Research work was also recommended before policy formation for Corporate Social Responsibility. Furthermore, research findings must be kept in mind when the policy is framed; policy must be target-oriented because it leads to the effectiveness of CSR policy and helps in goal achievement.
- It was experienced that most organizations include only those areas or factors of community developments that are directly or indirectly beneficial for the organization

They mostly ignore the fundamental problems of society. This practice was against the ethics of Corporate Social Responsibility. For the development of Community and Society, organizations must follow the ethics of Corporate Social Responsibility.

- Results show that the legal obligation of the Companies acts 2013 impacts CSR activities performance. So, in this way, Governments may also define the specific area for Corporate Social Responsibility according to the requirement. They must fix the accountability of organizations also.
- Results of the study show that some internal challenges of the organization and some external forces of the Community and business environment negatively impact the performance of CSR activities, so it has been recommended that business organization diagnoses the internal system of functioning and take corrective action if required. In the same way, Governments must also ensure a healthy business environment to improve the ease of doing global business ranking, reduce political interference, provide a healthy competitive market, provide an effective economic system and try to minimize all threats.
- Governments and Business organizations may create a model like a joint venture in which they include Experts, Governments Representatives, Organizations Representatives, and Representatives of Selected communities who take views and suggestions during policy formation. Moreover, CSR effectiveness could be increased by assigning work responsibility to the community under expert supervision.

5.8.2 Policy-Related Recommendations

On the basic interpretation of this study's results and findings, a few policies-related recommendations may be beneficial for the 'Business organizations, Employees and Community people.' The present study was about how Corporate Social Responsibility activities impact community development. So, there were a few dimensions of CSR, and a few community-related policy recommendations were made by organizations, policymakers, and government policy makers. There was a need for sustainable and systematic efforts from the side of policymakers to improvise the effectiveness of the policies and business environment. Some of the policy recommendations are as follows:

Recommendations for Improvement of the Education System

Developing Community and society as a whole, there was a need for a sound education system because education was only thin, which developed society and individuals. However, in the selected area (MP &CG), the research literacy rate was near about 80%, with male literacy at approximately 78% and female literacy at approximately 60%(Census,2011). It shows a positive trend compared to the census 2001, but that is not enough. So, there was a need for policy reconstruction regarding education and more results-oriented policies expected from the organization's policymakers of CSR activities and the Government's policymakers.

Recommendations for Improvement of Gender Equality

Equality based on gender is a significant indicator of societal development. Development of Society or Community development was not only related to Infrastructural Development, but it also deals with some values and ethics like Equality based on caste, religion, gender, etc. Justice for all, there must be democratic values. Present study results show that there was inequality in society based on gender. In this study, only 37% of valid Responses were received from females, and about 40% of females were employed in organized sectors. So, there was a need for change in policies regarding employability, education, training and development, socio-cultural values, and orientation of people also needed change In this way, CSR policymakers must keep these issues from policies in mind.

Recommendations for CSR Policy Making

There were few recommendations for the policy-making procedure of CSR activities. In policy-making, Organizations may include the expert's views and research reports and may take the insights from the Community people. The organization may increase the accountability of employees related to CSR activities; they may introduce reward and punish policy in CSR. Organizations may create a group and take responsibility for Community development according to their expertise. Corporate Social responsibility must treat as other activities of the organizations like Sales, marketing, and Finance.

Recommendations for Employees Training for CSR

Training and orientation of the employees play a crucial role accomplishment of a goal, and Training stimulates the improvement in employees and organizations. However, in the present study and the Indian Scenario, most organizations and employees do not feel the requirement for special training in Corporate Social Responsibility. However, it was recommended that employees have specific Skills and Knowledge of Social work for Corporate Social Responsibility activities. Training of employees must be helpful in the improvement of CSR results and effectiveness.

Recommendations for Legal Compliance

India was the first country in the world to make CSR activities compulsory and introduced the provisions in sec.135 of the Companies act 2013 and revised the Companies act 2019 to improve CSR activities. There were many provisions for the company's criteria, imprisonments, and fines. However, all those provisions were only targeted for the spending of CSR funds; they did not talk about where it was spent. In this way, organizations only focus on the spending of funds; they are less curious about the results and impact of the spending. Different kinds of Society and Region have different issues, and different kinds of companies have different skills. SO, Government must take the insights of area-specific issues and make provisions accordingly, and they may also supervise CSR activities, make provisions for motivation, and provide expected assistance. This way, CSR activities play a more critical role in Community Development.

Recommendations for Employment Creation

Unemployment is a significant issue for community development as well as for the nation also. In the selected area (MP& CG) of research, the Unemployment rate was very high, according to Madhya Pradesh economic survey data. About 30 lakh youth in 2021 were unemployed, and more than 90% were educated. As data shows that unemployment is a grave issue, there are many reasons behind this kind of unemployment like high population, low industrialization, Traditional Agriculture, Unskilled Youth, Outdate education system, lack of supportive entrepreneurial environment, and many more. So, Business organizations must keep this issue when formulating CSR policy. The organization may introduce many programs through CSR like Skill enhancement programs, Training & Orientation programs, and Internship programs. They can also promote small entrepreneurs by providing proper training and assistance. The government may also change the education policy and include skill enhancement training with education, provide financial and legal assistance to local entrepreneurs, develop tourist destinations and religious destinations, and establish modern industries like IT, war equipment, and robotics.

Recommendations for Entrepreneurial Development

Developing an entrepreneurial spirit is essential for society and the nation's development. Many developed and emerging countries have significant chunks of MSMEs, China was the best example, but in the Indian scenario, there was a lack of entrepreneurial spirit and environment. In the selected area of research, the population lived in Hilly and forest area, and they depend on forest natural resources are enriched with precious natural products, and have unique skills. However, they are compelled to live in poor conditions just because of their entrepreneurial spirit and environment. It is required for the organizations to provide them with modern marketing, management, production, and packaging skills and may provide financial knowledge and assistance through their CSR activities.

Government launches many insufficient programs like Skill India, Stand Up India, Make in India, MUDRA Yojana, and others. The government may adopt a global policy for marketing local and heritage products. Also, recognize the traditional art and culture and marketize them. The government may provide skill and financial assistance to SHGs with an organized marketing channel.

Recommendations for Nature Preservation

In the selected area of research, most organizations directly or indirectly depend on natural resources. Few are involved in the coal business, few in extracting other natural resources, and some are related to the cement industry, which also depends on natural resources. So, the population of the study also depended on natural resources, and during the study, the researcher realized that most industries do not follow the guideline. They exploit natural resources in unorganized ways that create a problem ecosystem and affect human lives. So, in this way, it's essential to adopt a sound policy for utilizing natural resources and the policy for Nature Preservation through CSR activities.

Governments may also fix the accountability of Organizations regarding Nature preservation and adopt and develop techniques like Carbon accounting and green accounting.

5.9 CONCLUSION OF THE STUDY

This study was about How Corporate Social Responsibility activities impact Community Development? To find the answer to this question was done. Research questions were farm in the study, and objectives were identified. Then null hypothesis was farmed, data was analyzed through statistical tools, and interpretation was made in the previous chapter. On behalf of results & interpretation, certain conclusions of the study were derived. Those are fallows:

- In this research, a total of 600 samples were found valid, including 300 community members from the selected area. And 300 from the employees of the Business organization. In the community sample, 63 % were male-female was 37% found valid.
- In the Community sample, about 50% were between the ages of 20 to 40, and about 5% were more than 60 years old. This way, the research tries to get people's insights from each age group.
- Of community members, about 2 % have matric education, 25 % were intermediates, nearly 45% were graduates, and more than 25% have master's degrees.
- Among the employees, approx. 40% was female approx. 60% were male, which shows gender inequality in employment.
- In this study, out of 300 employee respondents in the 20-30 age group, 3%, 30-40age group, 41.3%, 40-50 age group, 40.3 %, and 50-60 age group, 15.3% were recorded.
- In the data set, the foreman was 119, which is 39.7% of the total sample size, and lower-level management employees were 121which is 40.3% of the total sample size, and from the middle level of management, 32 employees, which is 10.7% of the total sample size and from the upper level of management is, 28 which is 9.3% of total sample size was recorded.
- Year of Experience was a significant factor in the socio-demographic profile of employees because experience matters in analyzing the circumstances of Corporate Social Responsibility (CSR), especially after the companies act 2013 and before the act. What was the preference and mode of functioning before and after the act? In this way the researcher can also understand the organization's challenges regarding CSR. So, the researcher tried to cover a reasonable sample size of each group in terms of the experience. In that process total sample size is 300

with which 0-8 years of experience16(5.3%), 8-16 years of experience, 78(26%), 26-24 years of experience73(24.3%), 24-32 year of experience77(25.7%) and 32-40 year of experience56(18.7%) was covered.

- This study used two scales for the data: one for employees and the second for Community members. Then reliability was measured through Cronbach alpha 'α' with the help of SPSS. The alpha value for both Scales was found to be significant.
- Normality test was done through analysis of skewness, kurtosis, and with Z Score value. Moreover, Sample distribution fulfills the assumptions of the doctrine of statistics regarding normality.
- CSR activities of corporate organizations predict the variables of Community development, i.e., Youth development, upliftment of underprivileged communities, and nature preservation. It has required changing the policies of implementation, policies of priorities, they also train and motivating employees towards CSR activities, and they may conduct research for other causes.
- Corporate branding predicted the performance of Corporate Social Responsibility activities by 7.4%. That means Corporate Branding was the driving factor for CSR activities performance.
- Honour & Awards predicted the performance of Corporate Social Responsibility activities by 23.6%. It seems that recognition significantly on the performance of Corporate Social responsibility.
- Training And awareness of employees predicted performance of Corporate Social Responsibility activities by 3.2%. Analysis shows that there was a need for more specific training of employees regarding CSR.
- CSR Implementation policy predicted the performance of Corporate Social Responsibility activities by 10.7%. That

indicates implementation procedure impact significantly.

- Legal Compliance predicted Corporate Social Responsibility activities performance by 52.3%, which means the Companies act 2013 impact positively on CSR performance.
- There were several challenges of internal and external environment like Community pressure, legal pressure, financial crisis, legal compliance, and many more those were responsible for the negative impact on the performance of CSR activities.
- H01 "*There exist no significant role of corporate social responsibility activities on community development.*" was **rejected**. That means Corporate Social Responsibility Activities are Significantly responsible for Community Development.
- H02: "*Business Environment Variables does not significantly impact on CSR activities of the organization.*" was **rejected**. The analysis reflects those internal and external variables of the business environment like Honour & Awards, Corporate branding, Training And awareness of employees, Legal Compliance, etc., responsible for CSR activities performance and effectiveness.
- $H_0$3: "*Challenges do not impact the delivery of CSR activities in community development.*" was **partially rejected**. That means some challenges of the Business environment significantly impact CSR activities performance, and some are not significant.
- Based on the results and interpretation of the study and the researcher's experience during the study, some suggestion and policy recommendation was made for the policymakers of the Organization regarding CSR activities, and Recommendations was made for Government policy maker for Community Development.

5.10 LIMITATIONS OF THE STUDY

Research work of this study was done through inevitable ups and downs of the situations at various levels, and there were particular reasons behind it like Scarcity of Resources, Time constraints, Knowledge and experience of the researcher, Geo-graphic locations of Organizations and Communities, Socio-cultural limits, and many more.

Due to Covid 19 pandemic, Data were collected through telephonic interviews, Google forms, and other electronic resources, so the researcher tried to minimize the errors, but it cannot be generalized that the data was 100% accurate.

Two districts of Madhya Pradesh and 2 Districts of Chhattisgarh were Selected for Study. Most of the Community belongs to Tribal communities, and they live in small, underdeveloped villages in forest and hilly areas. So, it cannot be generalized to other districts of MP &CG or the whole nation due to geographical and socio-cultural aspects.

This study considered limited variables of Community development and Corporate Social Responsibility for research. Other variables like Government policies may consider in future research.

In this research, only CSR was considered for Community development, and there may be other variables like Government policies, education status of Society,0Geographical location, and entrepreneurial activity. These variables should be considered in the future for research.

References

1. Idemudia, U. (2007). *Corporate social responsibility and community development in the Niger Delta, Nigeria: A critical analysis* (Doctoral dissertation, University of Lancaster).
2. Ismail, M. (2009). Corporate Social Responsibility and its role in community development: An international perspective. *Journal of International social research*, 2(9).
3. Eweje, G. (2006). The role of MNEs in community development initiatives in developing countries: Corporate social responsibility at work in Nigeria and South Africa. *Business & society*, 45(2), 93-129.
4. Ismail, M., Alias, S. N., & Rasdi, R. M. (2015). Community as stakeholder of the corporate social responsibility programme in Malaysia: outcomes in community development. *Social Responsibility Journal.*Ismail, M., Alias, S. N., & Rasdi, R. M. (2015). Community as stakeholder of the corporate social responsibility programme in Malaysia: outcomes in community development. *Social Responsibility Journal.*
5. Wilson, T. A. (2012). Supporting social enterprises to support vulnerable consumers: the example of community development finance institutions and financial exclusion. *Journal of consumer policy*, 35(2), 197-213.
6. McLennan, S., & Banks, G. (2019). Reversing the lens: Why corporate social responsibility is not community development. *Corporate Social Responsibility and Environmental Management*, 26(1), 117-126.
7. Trendafiova, S., Ziakas, V., & Sparvero, E. (2017). Linking corporate social responsibility in sport with community development: An added source of community value. *Sport in Society*, 20(7), 938-956.

8. E. Ite, U. (2004). Multinationals and corporate social responsibility in developing countries: a case study of Nigeria. *Corporate Social Responsibility and Environmental Management*, 11(1), 1-11.

9. Newell, P. (2005). Citizenship, accountability and community: the limits of the CSR agenda. *International affairs*, 81(3), 541-557.

10. Fisher, K., Geenen, J., Jurcevic, M., McClintock, K., & Davis, G. (2009). Applying asset-based community development as a strategy for CSR: A Canadian perspective on a win–win for stakeholders and SMEs. *Business ethics: A European review*, 18(1), 66-82.

11. Kapoor, G. K., & Dhamija, S. (2017). Mandatory CSR spending—Indian experience. *Emerging Economy Studies*, 3(1), 98-112.

12. Eilbirt, H., & Parket, I. R. (1973). The Corporate Responsibility Officer: a new position on the organization chart. *Business Horizons*, 16(1), 45-51.

13. Drucker, P. F. (1984). Converting social problems into business opportunities: The new meaning of corporate social responsibility. *California Management Review* (pre-1986), 26(000002), 53.

14. Singh, P., & Sarkar, S. (2017). Revolutionising Corporate Social Responsibility in India: Is It Truly Revolutionised?. *Asia-Pacific Journal of Management Research and Innovation*, 13(1-2), 1-12.

15. Wood, D. J. (1991). Toward improving corporate social performance. *Business Horizons*, 34(4), 66-74.

16. Jones, T. M. (1995). Instrumental stakeholder theory: A synthesis of ethics and economics. *Academy of management review*, 20(2), 404-437.

17. Friedman, M. (2007). The social responsibility of business is to increase its profits. *In Corporate ethics and corporate governance* (pp. 173-178). Springer, Berlin, Heidelberg.

18. Shah, S., & Bhaskar, A. S. (2010). Corporate social responsibility in an Indian public sector organization: A case study of Bharat Petroleum Corporation Ltd. *Journal of Human Values*, 16(2), 143-156.

19. Adewuyi, A. O., & Olowookere, A. E. (2010). CSR and sustainable community development in Nigeria: WAPCO, a case from the cement industry. *Social Responsibility Journal.*

20. Mukherjee, A. (2012). Corporate social responsibility of Banking companies in India: At cross roads. *International Journal of Marketing, Financial Services & Management Research*, 1(4).

21. Das, S. C. (2013). Corporate social reporting and human resource disclosures: experiences from insurance companies in India. *Social Responsibility Journal.*

22. Tiwari, U. (2014). Corporate Social Responsibility (CSR): A case study on NTPC Vindhya Nagar, Singrauli (MP) India. *Abhinav National Monthly Refereed Journal of Research in Commerce & Management*, Published by: Abhinav Publication, 3(10), 34-41.

23. Ghosh, S. (2014). A study of the participation of the private sector companies of India in corporate social responsibility activities through conjoint analysis. *Vision*, 18(2), 91-108.

24. Verma, A., & Kumar, C. V. (2014). An analysis of CSR expenditure by Indian companies. *Indian Journal of Corporate Governance*, 7(2), 82-94.

25. Atale, N., & Helge, E. J. (2014). Proposed framework for government of India to effectively monitor mandatory CSR initiatives of public sector Enterprises in India. *Journal of Human Values*, 20(1), 75-83.

26. Seriki, O. O. (2020). Looking through the African lenses: a critical exploration of the CSR activities of Chinese International Construction Companies (CICCs) in Africa. *International Journal of Corporate Social Responsibility*, 5(1), 1-9.

7. Amin, C., & Lastanti, H. S. (2020). PENGARUH CORPORATE SOCIAL RESPONSIBILTY TERHADAP PROFITABILITAS DAN VALUE CREATION DENGAN GOOD CORPORATE GOVERNANCE SEBAGAI VARIABEL MEDIASI. *Jurnal Akuntansi Trisakti*, 7(2), 339-364.

8. Aprianti, D. I., & Reonald, N. (2019). IMPLEMENTASI CORPORATE SOCIAL RESPONSIBILTY THE BODY SHOP INDONESIA SEBAGAI STRATEGI PASAR. *Jurnal Ekonomika: Manajemen, Akuntansi, dan Perbankan Syari'ah*, 8(1).

9. Slavova, I. (2013). Strategic perspective of corporate social responsibility. *Economic Alternatives*, 7(3), 90-105.

10. Demirel, A. (2020). CSR in sport sponsorship consumers' perceptions of a sponsoring brand's CSR. *International Journal of Sports Marketing and Sponsorship.*

11. Tsene, L., & Briana, M. (2019). CSR Wave: Social Impact as a Spillover Effect of a Brand's Crisis Communication Strategy–The Case of Lidl Hellas. *In Cases on Corporate Social Responsibility and Contemporary Issues in Organizations* (pp. 299-312). IGI Global.

12. Nwagbara, U., & Belal, A. (2019). Persuasive language of responsible organisation? A critical discourse analysis of corporate social responsibility (CSR) reports of Nigerian oil companies. *Accounting, Auditing & Accountability Journal.*

13. Duca, I., & Gherghina, R. (2018). CSR Initiatives: An Opportunity for the Business Environment. *In Ethics and Decision-Making for Sustainable Business Practices* (pp. 187-202). IGI Global.

14. Hawes, C., & Young, A. (2019). The Dao of CSR: Towards a Holistic Chinese Theory of Corporate Social Responsibility. *European Journal of East Asian Studies*, 18(2), 165-204.

15. Abdelhalim, K., & Eldin, A. G. (2019). Can CSR help achieve sustainable development? Applying a new assessment model

to CSR cases from Egypt. *International Journal of Sociology ar Social Policy.*

36. Mundakir, M. (2018, December). SUSTAINABLE BUSINES DEVELOPMENT THROUGH CSR IMPLEMENTATIO AT PT. HEINZ ABC INDONESIA. In ICCD (Vol. 1, No. pp. 512-517).

37. Marco-Fondevila, M., Moneva Abadía, J. M., & Scarpellini, (2018). CSR and green economy: Determinants and correlatic of firms' sustainable development. *Corporate Social Responsibili and Environmental Management*, 25(5), 756-771.

38. Sarmila, M. S., Zaimah, R., Lyndon, N., Azima, A. M., Saad, & Selvadurai, S. (2013). The Roles of Government Agency Assisting CSR Project for Community Development: Analys from the Recipients Perspectives. *Asian Social Science*, 9(8), 17.

39. Siddiq, S., & Javed, S. (2014). Impact of CSR on organization performance. *European Journal of Business and Manageme* 6(27), 40-45.